Bulimia: Hunger for Freedom

My spiritual journey of recovery

Katie Gesto

Copyright © 2004 by Katie Gesto

Bulimia: Hunger For Freedom
by Katie Gesto

Printed in the United States of America

ISBN 1-594676-46-1

Unless otherwise indicated, Bible quotations are taken from The New American Bible, Catholic Bible Press, Copyright © 1987.

www.xulonpress.com

Dedication

I dedicate this book in thanksgiving to the Loving One
who healed me and set me free
to live for Him alone.

Table of Contents

Introduction

You can be totally free from the grips of an eating disorder.

Sound impossible? This bold assertion is certainly disputed within mental health and medical circles. Many argue that similar to alcoholism, once you've struggled with bulimia, you'll never cease to fight the urge to purge.

Ask yourself right now, what do you believe in the depths of your soul? Do you think that total recovery is impossible?

I believe that God promises more for His children. When I started to put this belief into practice, my life began to change. I was a skid-roe bulimic for over ten years, feeling that life didn't exist beyond the porcelain bowl. Fearful I would be forever signed with a scarlet letter of insanity, my only hope for freedom seemed to be death itself.

Yet there was a spark of hope still alive and serve as a nurse missionary. One day I finally said to God, "For me to pursue my life-long dream of doing medical missionary work overseas, You have to totally heal me." Ten years later, I still find myself in awe that I eventually made it out of that horrifying maze of darkness. My life is now a total contrast to that life of chaos and pain.

Popular psychological theory supports the idea that eating disorders arise from a combination of long-standing psychological, interpersonal, and social conditions, and a connection to genetic sources is under investigation. Christian recovery circles tend to support these dimensions, but believe that a spiritual healing and a surrender to God can help one to be totally set free from the addiction to food and the roots of the disorder. I am living proof of this as my life now sings a sweet truth: freedom from bulimia is really possible.

If you are struggling with an eating disorder and you've run out of hope, you may need to get honest with God. You may need to admit that you've not been seeing your life clearly. Perhaps your eyes are worn from years of tears and disappointment from not yet overcoming the battle. Your heart may be hardened and you may feel too tired to try again. Don't put on a facade any more because it really won't get you anywhere. If your conception of God is distorted because bitter destructive thinking has tarnished you, begin to look at it. Get real with yourself. The God who created you has a specific plan and purpose for your precious life. Don't give up your struggle to overcome your eating disorder.

I wrote these pages in hopes that it could help you to do just that.

In this book I candidly describe the struggles and insights that have been key to my recovery. If you still wonder whether there's more work ahead in order to achieve a deeper recovery - lasting freedom—this story is for you. It won't be easy to read. I may say things that will pierce your heart, make you sad, angry, or defensive. Yet my prayer is that the Holy Spirit will use my journey to break strongholds in you, and to heal any wounds that keep you from being totally free of your eating disorder.

Though I have tailored this book to those who struggle with eating disorders, I hope that others will read it too. If you have a friend, family member, client, patient, or student who suffers from an eating disorder or another addiction, these pages will hopefully provide you with an understanding of what an addiction such as bulimia is like from the inside out. Afterwards, I hope you will be better equipped to assist, empathize, and pray for the complete healing of the people that you love and serve.

To all readers: Be open. Ask for the strength to ride the wave of healing.

CHAPTER 1

A Typical Day

This is a narration of what I experienced on a daily basis. It's a glimpse of the inner chaos that swarmed my mind for many, many years.

I wake up this Saturday morning in my University of Utah dorm room with a horrible but typical panicky feeling. It's not the anxious feeling that would be normal for the starting setter of the University of Utah's Division 1 Volleyball team who is facing one of the biggest games of the season this evening against Colorado State. No, this athlete's prevalent thought is, *I want to binge and purge!*

My mind is swarming with ideas of how to make the next procurement of food possible such as, *I'll go to the machines and get three candy bars and a cookie—No. I'll make pancakes and eat ice cream so that it all slides out easily when I vomit...No that takes too long!* It's too early to be thinking such things, but this is my life as a bulimic—a typical day for me.

I spring out of bed toward the kitchen searching for binge food while thinking, *I know! I'll go to the cafeteria and eat a bunch of donuts. It's Saturday and my friends won't be there, so I can gorge without anyone really noticing. Then I can vomit.* I shovel seven of my roommate Nancy's cookies into my mouth, thus finishing the box.

I always get worried that people will notice their food missing so I plan some time today to walk to the store to buy another box for her and eat the exact number that were already missing. A bulimics got to plan well if you want to hide this awful problem.

While I am walking over to the cafeteria for breakfast, I panic: *Those six cookies will probably digest by the time I finish eating in the cafeteria! I've got to get rid of them!* Finding the nearest toilet, I get rid of most of it. *Well, that's about 250 calories for the day digested...only about 1000 left. Katie-you're horrible!*

Finally at the cafeteria, and making sure none of my close friends are there to notice my bingeing, I calculate my moves. I always try to be inconspicuous but it's kind of hard when I take two donuts, a large milk, and sugared cereal, and then go back for seconds. Everyone knows a skinny girl like me can't eat that much without getting fat. I sit in the corner alone and ate, of course in a dignified manner, so as to look normal. I slip two donuts in my pocket on the way out to finish off later.

I hurry home to purge. It is only an hour since I awoke and I've already purged twice. I hop back into my bed since I have a lot of time before the big game. It is like I have to hide myself in my bed because I know that if I get up and go near our kitchen, I'll do it again. It's inevitable for me. My mind is never at rest because I'm either fighting the thoughts to binge and purge, or planning ways to stay abstinent.

Let it be only that one time that I do it today...I have so much homework to do! Then as quick as a flash of lightning, the urge to purge rushes in. I can't control it. I quickly decide to go to the market with the excuse that I need to replace the roommate's cookies. *I won't binge there. I'll just buy the cookies.* (As if I really believe myself when I think that I won't binge at the market!)

After a quick jog down campus, I am at the market. The bulk food bins are my killing field. I can't resist eating from them. I eat a few of the bits of sweets from them, of course without paying, and then buy the cookies, a dozen donuts, and a gallon of ice cream and run home. I torment myself again with the barrage of criticism: *You stupid jerk—I hate you! I hate you! How could you do this again? You thief and sinner!*

It is only 10:30 AM, 6 ½ hours until warm up for the big game, and I am still consumed with the stupid food. *I'm sick.*

Nancy is in her room, so I have to be quiet about things. I replace her cookies while shoving down a few donuts and milk, carefully listening for her in case she hears me. Within ten minutes, half the ice cream is gone and most of the donuts. Our dorm room has a good toilet with a powerful flush, so there is no concerns that it would not flush like in other places; which meant that the food has to be fished out manually and put in the trash.

Sometimes there's a bit of relief from the crazy thoughts, and so finally, after vomiting for the third time this morning, some mental relief was obtained and I am able to get on with the day's homework. I put the empty cartons in my backpack so I could toss them in a public trash can and my roommates wouldn't suspect me.

Actually, on most days I eat a healthy lunch in order to get in some good nutrition between the binges so that I have energy to play volleyball. So, I am off to lunch at the caf', and at the end of lunch I wolf down some ice cream, since it's always easy to purge and still keep in the nutritious foods. After lunch I amazingly get a good three hours of study time in; maybe because I made myself sit in the library where there are no food machines.

At 4:30 I get ready for the game. I have to eat something for dinner, as the game usually goes until 9 or 10 PM. I sure hope that I won't purge before the game, since it really messes up my playing because my mind gets so scattered.

But I did of course. It's rare if I don't purge at a meal. *Katie, you're such a loser!* At least it was only the last part of the meal: all the sweets and ice cream and bread. Nonetheless, I slaughter myself with a lot of self-loathing thoughts.

I thought I could shake it all off at warm ups, but my mind is all twisted up. I could hear our Coach yelling, "Katie! What's with you? SET the BALL!" *Man, Katie! You shouldn't have purged all morning! I can't concentrate...I am so awful! If they only knew...*

The game was a tough one and we lost in three matches. Everyone else played great, except for me. I had good moments, but I just couldn't set well. My playing keeps getting worse and it is killing me to know that it all has to do with the bulimia and I can't stop it. *I'm going to end up on the bench at this rate.*

After losing the game I go over to my friend's house to relax. I hope that at least over there I won't purge. I had had enough of it all that day. *C'mon Katie, don't do it again.* We are watching a movie and I am so psyched that after one hour I haven't delved into the Coke and pretzels. *Mission accomplished—no purging for the last hour! This is going to be a good night. I'll go right to bed after the movie so as to not eat a bite.*

But now Jana brought out buttered popcorn. I can't resist. I am trying so hard in my mind to resist. I think about going home right away but after 15 minutes of inner struggle, I rationalize: *I can handle just a small handful... Well, one handful won't hurt. I deserve more and have worked it off today.* Now I'm ending up eating the whole bowl.

By 11:30 we all start to head home. I slowly walk home, debating if I should stop somewhere to purge. *Should I purge, or should I leave it in? But I am so fat; I can't leave it in! Tomorrow will be better. I'll have a fresh start tomorrow and not do it again...EVER!* I always wish that but it never happens. I find a bathroom near the dorm and purged.

Finally, I'm here in bed writing this. I read the Bible, prayed and tried to relax, but I can't. I can't even cry, though I want to. *God, help tomorrow to be better. I am so tired of this. I just want it to end. Somehow.* I guess both games were lost today.

****

This was a very typical day in my life as a bulimic. Some days I would binge and purge more often than that, other days, a little less. People who don't have bulimia may feel utterly exhausted after reading this, and even indignant that a person could have such a crazy and sick lifestyle.

But to you who have bulimia or another addiction, you undoubtedly identify all too well. Yet the true anguish of such a lifestyle is known only to the soul who endures such a hell, and of course to the God who walks this journey with us. This seemingly silent partner in the struggle, God, is never without hope and grace for the one who suffers.

CHAPTER 2

My Story:
How It all Began

When someone learns that I was bulimic they inevitably ask, "What caused it?" Our human nature searches for concrete reasons as to why we suffer, and what causes our bad habits. If we can point our finger at specific causes we feel in control and able to fix them. In my case, and many others whom I have spoken to who have struggled with an addiction like bulimia, there are many presumed contributors, not just one person or experience that one could point their finger at. Certainly an undiscovered or lost sense of self encompasses many of the root causes.

The bottom line is that whether the causes are due to family issues, personal weaknesses, social pressures and/or traumatic experiences, we have a serious problem and we have to dig through the rubble to heal the wounds.

Without casting blame upon anyone or any other factors, I will share with you my story.

Born and raised in body-beautiful southern California, I loved playing sports. Weight consciousness was part of the game, both on the courts and in my family. I picked up what the media and the culture told me about how I should look and relate to the people around me in order to be desirable. At times, regrettably, the men in my life verbally affirmed that tarnished view.

Before I became bulimic, I acquired the family nickname of "garbage disposal" and "bird legs" since I could eat anything and still look like a twig. I loved to eat. On Saturdays would polish off eight or ten of my father's pancakes before going out to shoot hoops with him.

When I was twelve, my body-image problems began. Although they were not overweight, my mother and sister often complained about their "childbearing hips," in between bites of cookies. I was thinner than both of them so I figured that I had nothing to worry about.

In the eighth grade, my best friend, Desiree, shared with me her fear of being fat. We weighed ourselves one afternoon. The scale stopped for me at 108 pounds: three more than Desiree. Her satisfaction about weighing less caused me to panic. I screamed within, "I'm fat!"

From that point on, I began eating less and watching my weight. I tried to diet for two days, but couldn't stand it, so I gave up. In the back of my mind a voice kept resounding, *I am fat!* My inherited childbearing hips suddenly seemed to erupt, and the fat on my stomach seemed enormous even though in reality I had not physically changed much.

At thirteen, I went to an all girls' college prep school. My parents were going through some hard times, which added to my inner restlessness. I was anxious to find friends, and I was in need of people whom I didn't have to compete with about weight issues. I was always well-liked, but it took a lot of time for me to develop close friendships. Happily, new friends came quickly due to my participation in sports. I cut down on the amount I was eating since my body was definitely changing shape and I was afraid of getting fat. I became more conscious of my body image as the numbers steadily rose on the scale. Nevertheless, I was still very thin and muscular. I didn't realize that with the growth in height and figure the increase in weight was healthy.

As I tried controlling the scale, things became more intense at home. It was difficult to handle the escalating arguments between my parents. My mother would yell about my father's drinking habits, wanting him to change. Dad would then complain about mom's complaining. It seemed like a continuous cycle. A constant underlying tension that friends even noticed ran through our home. I felt less secure at home and at school. There were no fists flying, foul language, or degrading things said to me, yet I hated any conflict and lack of peace. At times I'd hide in my bedroom closet and cover my ears so I couldn't hear my parents arguing.

Compared to other families, our situation was very mild. Yet for me, being such a sensitive teenager, it hurt to have disunity in my family. I buried the hurt deep within me. Although my parents were supportive and helped me to develop morally and spiritually, I wasn't able to totally relax and share my thoughts and concerns with them. I was angry with both of my parents and somehow felt responsible yet helpless to fix their problems.

One night at the end of my freshman year I saw my mom crying and it scared me. *If mom is this broken from all the unrest, whom can I lean on? Who will be the rock and stability in this home?* I went to bed with tears in my eyes and vowed: I will never hurt my Mom like Dad and the others have. I will support her and stay good. I was unaware that soon I would be in the grips of a disease that would deeply hurt my Mom and family in ways I'd only understand later in life.

The Beginnings of bulimia

It was Thanksgiving of my sophomore year. I was especially full after Grandma's delicious cheesecake and my stomach was bulging beyond its allotted limit. "I feel like throwing up, I feel so full," I joked to my mom. She gave me a look that said she knew I wouldn't do such a thing and replied sarcastically, "Well then, go ahead!" With hidden defiance in my step I walked to our bathroom and secretly vomited. I didn't even have to put my finger down my throat but just bent over and it all released. Actually, I have never even heard of someone forcing themselves to vomit after eating too much and bulimia was a foreign word.

After it was over I thought, *That was wonderful! My stomach feels a lot better. I can now go eat another piece!* I knew it wasn't right but I ignored the guilt and cleaned up the dishes by eating and vomiting another time. In those days, bulimia was neither talked about nor had I ever heard of it; nonetheless I discovered it.

A week later, after feeling full, the thought taunted me: I wouldn't gain weight if I vomited after I ate—I could keep my weight under control. After dinner, while washing the dishes, I vomited in a salad bowl and ran it through the garbage disposal.

Fear ran down my spine. Something was not right. What if my parents or sisters found out or heard me, or walked in? I knew if they discovered my secret, they would be outraged and disgusted. I developed a technique that kept my purging quiet and hidden. I felt ashamed for vomiting, yet, for some strange reason, I felt relieved when I ate and vomited. There was something about it that felt good.

The pattern continued and went from once a week to three times a week.

Before long I was purging every day, then twice a day. Soon I was purging up to four or five times daily. On school days and weekends, my spare time would be consumed with bingeing and purging up to eight times. I would purge for any reason, and often for seemingly no reason at all.

After several months, the bulimia became a sort of "friend", as sick as that is. It was a replacement for interacting with others and a distraction from thinking about my family situation. I had never learned to verbally communicate my feelings. I had a lot of friends growing up, and some very close ones, but did not confide in them. Nor did I share much with my family. It seemed impossible to say to someone, "You know, I am having a terrible day. I really feel sad about the way things are going in my life. I am really hurting". Bulimia was that friend.

My unidentified feelings became buried one on top of the other. When I was sad or lonely I'd binge and purge; when my parents would fight, or my sister would yell at or ignore me, I'd binge and purge. If I felt good, or felt nothing at all, food became the way of processing my positive feelings too. Everything could be going well when, like a flash flood, the urge would come and I'd run to the toilet. I despised the parts of me that felt insecure, out of control, angry, and disappointed. I didn't want to show anyone that I was needy, or worse: that I was hurt. These were things that I couldn't even acknowledge myself.

Even if I had been aware of these feelings and made the connection that if I talked about them I wouldn't feel like purging, I would have had no idea how to express what I felt in words. I had never done that before. I was stuck.

Admitting the Problem

By the spring of my junior year of high school I was definitely caught in the whirlwind of bulimia. One day I revealed my horrible secret to my best friend, Mary. She promised not to tell any friends or coaches, but after realizing how severe it was, she dragged me to the school counselor. Mrs. Stayner took me under her wing. After a few meetings she told me that I needed professional help. I candidly agreed, almost with a sense of joy and relief. She continued, "And you're going to have to tell your Mom."

I panicked. I pleaded. "I CAN'T tell her!" I cried as the tears rolled down my gaunt face—tears that had not been shed since I made that vow my freshman year to never hurt my mom. She took me in her arms and held me.

This was going to be the hardest thing I had ever done.

That night, I asked my mom to tuck me in. As she sat with me on the bed I said, "Mom, I need to talk. Mom, every once in a while, I eat too much and....I throw up. Mrs. Stayner, the counselor at school, thinks I need to see a psychologist so it doesn't develop into a bigger problem."

She said, "Honey, whatever you need to do, that's okay. Dad and I will support you and will pay for whatever. Don't worry, Kato." I didn't tell her the full truth because I was afraid to admit how severe the problem really was. I was afraid of placing more burdens on my mother, and afraid of being vulnerable with my family. I had been the tough one who never complained and rarely cried. The one who had it all together.

Even though I can't remember my parents reinforcing that role, it was one that I naturally assumed. I was also afraid it would hurl me out of control. It was irrational, but I felt that if I admitted my weakness and how I felt broken in a hundred pieces, my family would truly have fallen apart. What I wasn't aware of was that I feared more the possibility of me falling apart. That is what I couldn't handle.

Mom called my school counselor and together they decided to send me to a psychologist who specialized in eating disorders. I was put through a series of blood tests and had weekly appointments for over a month, but because I didn't want my parents to keep paying for it, I told them that I could handle the problem on my own. I knew, however, that I needed more intense help than just a weekly visit with a therapist.

Looking back, I see that it would have been the best, though hardest, thing to tell my family about the severity of my bulimia and just how scared I actually was. My family probably would have gone with me to family counseling and I would have received more help that way. My athletics may have been affected and even postponed for a season, but since the bulimia adversely affected my college volley-ball career anyway, it would have been wise to begin this process in high school.

Another reason why I wasn't honest right from the start was because I was too proud. I thought I'd lose friends. I didn't want my image to be tarnished. Another girl in my sophomore class went through a hospital program for anorexia. At first we were all shocked and didn't know how to relate to her. Later we respected her because she had the courage to deal with the problem. I wish I too had had that courage.

The support and love I received from the school counselor, and my good relationships with the coaches and teammates, began to touch a part of me that was hurting: a part of me I didn't know I had. My parents were loving and supportive in their own way, but I was unable to fully receive from them.

While in counseling, I had an opportunity to speak with a woman in her twenties who had had bulimia for ten years. I thought to myself, *That pathetic woman! I can't believe what a wimp she is not to kick the habit of bulimia after her first few years! I will NEVER go that long! I can stop whenever I want...Oh God, I hope I will not be in it for that long, but what if I am?* It was too frightening to consider that possibility.

A year later, in my senior year, I was still in the thick of bulimia. I was tired of getting sick and positively wanted to stop. Although still unwilling to fully admit it, the momentum of the addiction was too strong to halt on my own strength.

One dark night while driving home from volleyball practice in my mother's car, I felt absolutely miserable. I was out of control, tired, desperate, and terrified. I suddenly wanted to drive off the edge of the overpass and kill myself—just end the entire mess. Thoughts swirled around my mind. *What if I hurt someone else on the road? I really don't want to wreck my mom's car, leaving that as my last mark on this world. I wonder if a week in the hospital might help me stop.* All I can say is that my guardian angel must have been working overtime because I made it home.

I was glad I hadn't killed myself. As hard as things were, I did want to get through this and live. Killing myself seemed like the easy way out, and the best punishment for what seemed like constant failure. No one wants to feel constantly out of control, to be exhausted every day from strategizing binges and purges.

As the end of my senior year approached I kept my composure; yet inside I knew I was in deep trouble. I spent time in the school chapel talking to the Lord, begging him to help me. I remember being in my living room, too much in pain to cry more than a few tears. I was kneeling down, beating on the floor and yelling, "God!! Help me get over this! I can't do this anymore! Help me!" I knew God must have the answer to this three year long problem. I knew His help was the key. Yet how that help would actually come, I didn't know.

I grew up in a supportive Catholic home and felt very close to God even as a child. With those good foundations of prayer and teaching, I cried out to God in this desperate time of my life to rescue me from the inner hell I was living.

Recovery Begins

I was blessed with a volleyball scholarship to the University of Utah in 1984. I thought that a fresh start and a break from the tensions in my home would help me to leave the bulimia in California.

The University of Utah was beautiful, and located near the mountains. It had a well-developed health sciences department, which would provide me with opportunities to investigate various majors. Although at first I was homesick, the excitement of being in a new place carried me through some of the sadness. Practices were tough—I had never worked out as hard as I did with the Utah volleyball team. I met a lot of good friends and enjoyed dorm-life.

For a while, the bulimia was in check. I couldn't binge and purge as often as before because I wouldn't be able to concentrate as well on my volleyball skills. The rigorous workout schedule allowed me to binge and not purge every so often without having any effect on my weight; but the pressure I put on myself to perform well was more intensified at the university level.

As soon as the volleyball season was over, the momentum of my bulimic cycles returned full force. The all-you-can-eat cafeteria and junk food machines became a prime medium for my addiction to flourish. Soon I was in the mouth of the monster again. I was disappointed and felt completely out of control. I didn't know where to turn.

I began looking at the counseling centers and support groups for eating disorders-anything that could help. I was afraid to contact a counselor because I didn't want my team to know I was seeing a "shrink". I kept putting it off, thinking, *It will go away; it's just the stress of a new place, new responsibilities....*

As I was walking down the halls of the Student Union one night, feeling horrible about myself, I saw a sign advertising a Campus Crusade for Christ film called "If I Should Die". The people looked friendly and inviting, and I wanted a touch of God. I walked in and sat down in the back, hoping to find a solution to my problems. The movie featured a couple who had died in a car accident. It challenged the viewers to ask themselves, "If I were to die, do I know where I would go?"

I sat in the back, hoping no one would see me. Then the words of Ephesians 2:8,9 flashed on the screen: "For by grace you have been saved through faith, and this is not from you; it is the gift of God; it is not from works, so no one may boast." It finally hit me: God wasn't keeping a tab of X's on one side and happy faces on the other.

I was blown away when I realized that God wanted to direct my life so personally and intimately. I wasn't actually meant to be the one totally in control. I had a Father who wanted to take that responsibility. Grace was meant to help me in my weakness so I could live the way I was meant to live.

I didn't know exactly what it meant for Christ to *control* my life, since I had always thought I had to steer the direction of where I was going, but deep down, something within me resounded, YES!

That night, I was given an opportunity to pray. This was my prayer:

> *Lord Jesus, thank You for dying on the cross for my sins. I want to repent for the ways in which I have offended You and gone away from where You were leading me. I want You to come into my heart and cleanse me from all of my sins and heal my wounded heart. I believe You have a plan for my life. Make me into the person You have created me to be. I dedicate my life to You and ask you to make me whole so that I can live in Your grace and know Your love for me. I want to come home to my family, the family of God. Thank You for coming into my life.*

Tears were streaming from my eyes as I finished that beautiful prayer because it expressed the deepest desire within my heart. I cried: *Lord, I know You are the answer to my bulimia. I give up. I allow You to do whatever you want in me. I know You are and always have been in my heart through the Sacraments and in my prayers all my life, but I didn't understand that You wanted to direct my life so intimately by Your grace.*

I thought I had to do it all. I continued praying, *I am really tired of directing my own life. I don't know how to really listen to You or follow You more intimately and it even scares me a bit. Please, in your perfect timing, stop this horror of bingeing and purging. I'm lost as to how to overcome this and I am really afraid, alone and very tired. Please do it in me!*

That night something within me changed. It had been so long since I had felt that joy and hope within me—new life within. I knew that this was the start of a new road towards recovery. From that night onward, I have never felt the pitted emptiness and severe loneliness that I had felt for so long.

A week later I began meeting with the leader from the Campus Crusade staff. She carefully walked me through many questions, concerns, and problems. I confided in her my secret of the bulimia. She became a constant support through all of my struggles.

Disappointedly, the struggle did continue despite my newfound strength. I thought God would instantly and painlessly free me from the bulimia and I would be instantly healed; but the long recovery process was only beginning. The difference was that after that night I felt for the first time I was battling toward recovery with a new hope lighting the way.

I met a fellow Californian who was attending Overeaters Anonymous 12-step meetings in Salt Lake City. Reluctantly I went to my first meeting and, although I felt uncomfortable being the only skinny person there, I felt like I fit in. I began to understand that being "powerless over food" opened the door for God's grace to heal the inner wounds causing the bondage to eating so that I could one day have freedom to eat with healthy control.

Finally, during my sophomore year, I received counseling for a few months from a woman in Salt Lake City. She taught me Scripture that steered me toward reforming of my mind, such as Romans 12:1,2: "I urge you therefore, brothers, by the mercies of God, to offer your bodies as a living sacrifice, holy and pleasing to God, your spiritual worship. Do not conform yourself to this age, but be transformed by the renewal of your mind, that you may discern what is the will of God, what is good and pleasing and perfect."

It was wonderful to see how Scripture viewed who I was in Christ! In 1986, just before my junior year began, I traveled to South America with the volleyball team of Athletes in Action (AIA): a branch of Campus Crusade for Christ. There, for six weeks in Peru, Bolivia, and Equator, our women's volleyball team traveled around sharing the Gospel before we played the national and college volleyball teams.

I was sure that the two-month opportunity for abstinence would cure me of my bulimia. I thought, *What kind of person would binge and purge on a Christian volleyball team?* Surely this would knock some sense into me before my junior season of volleyball. My athletic performance had deteriorated during my sophomore year and I was afraid to think how it would be the following year if the bulimia didn't stop.

Playing with AIA was such a gift. I met the nicest people and developed lasting friendships. On the team I felt unconditional acceptance and love. I didn't have to beat myself up if I did poorly, and I could lessen the pressure on myself to be perfect. I played terribly all six weeks, but the amazing thing was that the coach and the rest of the players weren't bothered by it. Although I binged a few times, I managed not to purge the entire two months, which was an incredible victory for me!

When my Utah season started again, I expected the hell to be all over and to play with my old spunk. I was elected Captain of the team and my hopes were high. The first week was great, but by the third week the new freshman setter was starting in my place and I was catching splinters on the bench. I was a wreck once again. My mind spun when I set, I couldn't concentrate, and I felt jittery inside. I had never been so humiliated.

At that point, I just wanted to die. It wasn't a suicidal plea, just a tired warrior's cry. I was so tired of fighting the big bully, bulimia. *Lord, just take me home. I want to go!*, I cried. I wanted to go to my heavenly home because it wasn't peaceful at my parent's home. Yet even in that place of exhaustion and humiliation there was a deep peace inside.

I was committed to getting help after the season finished. I was finally honest with my coach about how my bulimia was causing my poor performance and that I needed to be committed to recovery, whatever that meant. She understood. I knew that I would get better.

The Truth Comes Out

Christmas found me back in California. I hadn't shared with my family any of the turmoil I was going through, except for mentioning that I wasn't playing very well. I planned to tell my parents the full truth about my addiction after Christmas. My bulimia was inflamed while baking all of the holiday treats; yet I continued my secret purging.

Usually when I was with my family I could hide my feelings, but this time it was impossible. I was clinically depressed and could barely smile. I tried to disguise my depression by telling my family, "I'm just tired from this last semester." But I knew they knew something was really wrong.

On Christmas morning, after opening presents and eating brunch, my dear Mom tenderly said, "Kate, come over here and sit down with me." Cold fear flooded through me. I think she knows...Oh no! I walked over and sat down next to her, and she put her arm around me, embracing me close to her chest. "What's wrong, Kate? We've all noticed how depressed you've been; you're just not yourself. What's going on?" I gave her a look of "What do you mean what's wrong? There's nothing wrong!"

I couldn't hold back any longer. I dropped my head on her shoulder and began sobbing. She simply held me on her lap and cradled me. She was grieved to see her daughter so broken—something she had never witnessed before.

With relief, I began telling her the whole story from beginning to end. I told her how out of control I felt and that I couldn't stop. I was elated that I didn't have to hide anymore! She shared her sadness that none of the family knew the severity of it before this moment.

My parents supported me in dedicating the next semester to getting well. They assured me, "Whatever you need to do, we will support you." And they did.

My mother suggested giving up my scholarship because of the unnecessary pressure it might be inflicting on me. I had already considered that awful possibility, along with the humiliation accompanying such a decision. I told her that I would think about it, never thinking that it would have to come to that point. Yet deep down something told me it would happen.

I returned to Utah and took a road trip with Campus Crusade for Christ to Oregon for a New Year's conference with hundreds of other college youth. We prayed in the New Year, worshipping the Lord from our hearts. It was wonderful! I felt that the conference was what I needed to give myself a new start. It would help me to get myself shaped up and regenerated for the next semester and to finish my senior year of volleyball. *Could it be possible to have a year free from bingeing and purging?* I was hopeful.

One of the speakers at the conference spoke about our "Isaacs". He read from Genesis 12: the story of Abraham sacrificing his son, Isaac, to God. It required total trust and abandonment to God to sacrifice the one thing Abraham held dearest to his heart. Like Abraham, we were all challenged to leave our idols, sins and addictions on the altar and not let them jump back into our lives. I willingly placed my Isaac of bulimia on the altar. I certainly didn't want it anymore. I knew, like Abraham, that "trust and abandonment" were key to my recovery from bulimia and any other bondage.

The bulimia did return. Within a week after school started, I plummeted into a severe depression and a rage of purging. I couldn't handle my sixteen credits, so I dropped four. A week later, it was evident that I couldn't even handle that. Although on the outside I appeared to have it together, I was unable to concentrate on anything. I felt panicked and insecure, like the lid of my emotions was beginning to fly off. I couldn't seem to make any decisions and felt as if I were losing my mind. Just deciding what to wear that day was totally overwhelming. *What's wrong with me?* I had sincerely tried to give up the bulimia and make a new start. I did depend as best as I could on the Lord's help to stop bingeing and purging, yet I was even worse than before Christmas.

Things were quickly spiraling downward. *Why am I not well? Why are You delaying Your help, God?* I didn't understand, yet I still had a deep peace amidst my pain. I knew, somehow, I was being mysteriously carried through, even though the symptoms of the bulimia were raging and it seemed as though God had forgotten me.

The last straw came when, after only three weeks back at school, I had "eaten" all of my savings and spent January's one hundred-dollar monthly scholarship allotment on binge foods. Desperate, I called my parents to ask for help in finding a hospital. They were shocked at how badly I was doing. They now had to face the full reality of my situation.

The phone call was tense. The daughter who had always had it together now couldn't stop throwing up and needed a hospital? I could feel the pain in their voices. Dad called me a day later and he had found an eating disorder hospital in San Pedro, California based on the Twelve Steps of Alcoholics anonymous.

A week later, I had withdrawn from university and was on my way home. To some people, I didn't look like I needed an eating disorder hospital. Although I had gained about ten pounds in the last year in efforts to stop purging, I did not look noticeably overweight. To my friends I looked peaceful and in control, which to some extent was true, since I did trust that God was providing this opportunity. But the calmness was also due to the fact that I was numb inside and void of external emotions.

The six-week stay in San Pedro Hospital gave me an opportunity to begin learning how to feel feelings that I had stuffed down for so long with food. There were about eighteen of us living together in the hospital, mostly women. Our daily schedule provided us with group therapy sessions, nutrition classes, and exercise. It helped to be around others who understood the panic and difficulty in choosing what to eat in the cafeteria and at a restaurant. It felt awful to simply eat healthily. I met others who also had the temptation to over-exercise in order to lose weight, and who understood the awful feeling of simply "just living" inside your body. Although there were no scales there, I could tell I lost a few pounds that month which was nice.

My family drove one and a half-hours to participate in the evening family therapy sessions two times per week. As much as I had not wanted them involved, it was good for us to meet as a family to begin improving our communication skills. It took a lot of time for me to begin letting the iceberg of frozen feelings melt, particularly to share them with my family. With fear and trembling I began being honest about how weak I felt inside, and how vulnerable and broken I was. That was extremely painful to admit, yet it was a relief to do. I had never been aware of these deep feelings before!

The most memorable family session was the time our counselor asked my little sister how she felt about my bulimia. To my surprise, she broke down crying. She looked at me compassionately and said, "I am just really sad for her!" I couldn't believe it! I thought, *What's the big deal? Don't cry, Carrie.* I felt embarrassed that I was so cold in response to her heartfelt love for me. I didn't know what to say to her.

It was at that point that I began taking more responsibility for my bulimia because I saw how it affected others whom I loved. I could not rationalize, as before, that it was only hurting myself. My family was hurting for me but I never intended to cause them pain. I had to let them in and help me through this, even if it caused them more pain.

At the end of the six weeks, despite a few breakthroughs, I had not let down my guard emotionally. I was still afraid of the risk. Yet, the hospital team and I felt it was time for me to be discharged. I deeply hoped that these six weeks of abstinence would give me the motivation to not vomit again.

On the third day out, I ate a bunch of junk food, hoping to keep it down and suffer the fatty consequences. After battling the vicious temptations to purge for half a day, I rationalized, *Let me just do it one more time. It will make me remember how awful it is and it will calm any future raging thoughts of purging. Really, it will be best to just purge this right now. Plus, I have more control now with six weeks of abstinence.*

Needless to say, that was the beginning of three more years of bulimia. After leaving the hospital, I went home to live with my parents, returning to San Pedro Hospital twice a week for therapy sessions. The outpatient program continued for seven months and the groups helped me to practice expressing my feelings in a safe environment. I also attended Overeaters Anonymous, Alcoholics Anonymous (although I rarely drank, I liked their meetings) and Adult Children of Alcoholics meetings, along with some other bulimic support group meetings. Sometimes I would attend two meetings a day in order to keep myself from falling into a binge.

Later, I moved into a halfway house run by the Women's Aglow Fellowship. I was welcomed with open arms. The time alone and away from family and friends gave me time to reflect on my life. The biggest challenge in those years was to figure out what I was supposed to do with these feelings that often felt like live, hot wires. They often caused me pain, a pain that was of a different nature than the despair of bulimia.

At times, I felt as if I couldn't even move because I hurt so badly.

Often, I didn't even know why I was hurting—I just did. During support meetings, I would sometimes break out crying and other times I would feel insecure and out of control.

In 1988, after five months at the halfway house, I decided to finish my schooling at the Franciscan University of Steubenville, Ohio. I did not want to wait until I was perfectly recovered to get on with my life.

Healing Flows

Although the bingeing and purging continued to slowly diminish, I still struggled with it while living in the dormitories. Between classes, I had time to be quiet in the chapel, absorbing the healing grace that so freely poured into me. I couldn't see the healing, or often feel it, but I knew it was happening and I saw the fruit of it in that first year of school. I became more myself and more free and healed. I continued to uncover the root of my sick thinking, replacing it with truth about myself.

My first year of abstinence began while I was there. When I was 22, I joined a Franciscan religious community for two years while finishing my nursing degree. During my first year in the convent, I fell into a depression. It forced me to seek Christian counseling for over a year with an excellent counselor, Tom Laird. I saw him weekly and was supported by great sisters in the convent who loved me through my difficult inner work.

Tom showed me how to weave my psychological inner healing with my desire to pursue Gospel living. He said, "Katie, Jesus calls us to love one another passionately— everyone. That is the Gospel. If you are not able to do that to your parents, men and people who have hurt you, then it is keeping you from a deeper relationship with God and others. You need to look at the self-protective vices you have put up which prevent you from living the Gospel; repent and ask God to change you. I can help you to do this," he said. Although it meant a lot of pain, I consented to walk with God through this grueling path of healing which was a major breakthrough.

Some days I was broken inside and could only lay down and cry, letting the Lord do surgery on my wounded heart. The pounds I'd slowly gained over the years came off as I worked at breaking down barriers to intimacy with others and God.

I left the convent at 25 to pursue a lay missionary vocation and to be open to marriage. The transition was difficult and I fell back into vomiting for very short periods of time during that next year, but the devastating force to bulimia never returned. I never went back to it with the intensity I had in those first ten years because the main roots were healed.

After leaving the convent, whenever I was "stuck"

emotionally and not able to work through something, I would call Tom, my counselor, and talk things through with him. After the three years of abstinence the purging returned only for a few, short episodes for about two years after that. Then it finally ended until the present day. There was no specific day when I was able to say, "I am recovered", but as I continued to work through my problems and pain, I was freed.

My dream had always been to do missionary work overseas. At one point in college, I remember praying, "Lord, if you want me to do missions, you have to totally heal me of this. I can not do this kind of work and still be bingeing and vomiting. I believe you are calling me and I believe you will heal me of this!" I read Galatians 5:1 and felt God saying that He would set me free so that I can be who I am called to be, "For freedom Christ set us free; so stand firm and do not submit again to the yoke of slavery." And He has. And He will for you!

Since that season of recovery I have served for several years as a missionary in Sudan, Zambia, Brazil and Dominican Republic, many times under great duress, particularly in Sudan. The work of conversion, freedom from pride, vices and other character defects continues as it does for every human being until we die, but I no longer feel compelled to anything in the way I did when I was bulimic. That's a real healing!

I don't struggle with food any more. I can maintain my weight and eat whatever I want. My confidence lies in God's mercy and in His grace that I will stay recovered. I have developed many helpful tools over the years, which enable me to deal with my emotions, spiritual life, and physical body. Also, I have come to know and accept myself. I have confidence that I will continue to make the right choices and will not return to bingeing and purging. I have faced deep pain in my heart, and that now helps me to face other difficult issues, along with being a healing balm for others who are suffering.

It was a long road of ups and downs, starts and failures, but I can now say with great thanksgiving, that I am recovered from the grips of bulimia. It was worth the struggle! Glory to God!

CHAPTER THREE

Unraveling my Heart

During my first group therapy meeting at the San Pedro Hospital, we went around the room introducing ourselves and sharing our feelings. All I felt was nauseous and an ice cold panic through my body because I was so nervous to be vulnerable before strangers.

When my turn came, with sweating palms I calmly answered, "Hi, I am Katie, a bulimic, and I feel...ah... good." Jack, the therapist, looked at me somewhat amazed said, "Katie, 'good' is not a feeling. McDonald's hamburgers are 'good'. How are you *feeling*?"

It was a shocker to discover that 'good' was not a feeling! *Okay, if it's not*, I thought, *then what is a feeling?* Noticing my dumbfounded pause, Jack suggested a few possibilities, "Maybe you're feeling sad, scared, happy, overwhelmed...or numb?"

I had absolutely no clue. I guessed it was 'numb' because I wasn't experiencing any of those other feelings but I was too embarrassed to say that because I figured that that was a cop-out, so I said, "Yea—I'm feeling happy— happy to be here." I quickly motioned for him to move on to the next victim, trying to mask my utter humiliation and confusion. What *am* I feeling? I thought. The whole situation puzzled me.

Looking back, I have to laugh at myself. How can a person feel good and happy when they just had to give up their volleyball scholarship to move home, and then be admitted to an inpatient hospital for out of control eating habits? But, in a sense, I *was* happy to be there. For the first time, I knew that I was going to learn how to be real, and how to release the impacted layers of suppressed feelings that I had buried for two decades.

My feelings and emotions were disjointed, and I was completely out of touch with them. I wasn't able to identify anything. Even in my best moments I didn't know what I felt because I was so used to operating out of my head rather than my heart. This process caused me to operate in a constant anxiety state. My mind and body were always tense and on guard against letting me feel the feelings of the moment. I was constantly thinking about how to keep the secret of bulimia hidden. This caused an imbalance within my body, mind and spirit.

After years of avoiding feeling much of anything, my system became entirely stressed and couldn't even process every day emotions. It's similar to a car without an exhaust system: It is eventually going to clog itself up and ruin its own engine.

Unclogging the Drain

During those first few days in the hospital, I began learning about the new world of feelings. I was perplexed, yet overjoyed, to discover that it was possible for a person to feel two feelings at the same time. There were still other times that I felt scatterbrained, anxious and excessively sensitive, all at the same time, almost as if I were losing my mind! It was an exciting revelation for me!

Learning to feel was hard work. When I found myself filled with anxiety, numbness and wanting to binge, I had to work to think about what was going through my head and to talk myself through it. I learned that my pipes got clogged and the emotions could not move through and thus I needed to figure out what was bugging me.

At those times I would say, *Katie, slow down. What is wrong? You are not being present to others, yourself or God. What's up?* It usually turned out that something had happened recently that had put my emotions in a tether. I just hadn't wanted to face it or hadn't had time to think about it, so I unconsciously "checked out" for a while to avoid it. The problem was that if I didn't deal with what originally was bothering me, the emotions would build up and have to come out in another way, like bulimia or being un-loving toward others.

I hadn't realized that throughout high school and college I had been operating in that numbness most, if not all of, the day. I was too afraid to feel. As I began to see the connection of bulimia to clogged emotions, I began getting a glimpse of the big picture of recovery: Before I could work on good eating habits-which is the root of recovery-the room filled with blocked emotions must be unlocked.

Being a nurse, I have likened this numbed state to a condition I call, "emotional constipation". My definition: "Feelings experienced for the past months, or years, which get all confused, difficult to sort because they have been stuffed over and over, resulting in a clogged, numb emotional state masking inner pain and fear." If this condition goes on for too long, the result is feeling lost inside, not being able to concentrate on the task at hand, and an inability to connect with people. This person may still be able to say to a friend, "Oh, I understand." or, "I feel so sad for you." but they do not really *feel* sad or *feel* compassion. They can't.

The remedy is to unravel the web of emotions, and then learn to express them in a healthy way. I had to learn how to discover what I was feeling presently, but I also had to go back in time and feel the emotions from significant past events in order to remedy the emotional constipation.

When the lid from the long, seeded tangle of emotions is removed, pain follows. Feelings of deep hurt, disappointment and anguish that accompany certain memories are revived. It sometimes felt like a tidal wave gushing out on me, or like I was an electrical telephone wire just cut loose and frantically whipping itself around in the air. I must say, it was not pleasant; but it was necessary to go through. I was thawing from frostbite.

For those reading this, wait through the pain...it won't last forever.

I began learning various techniques to process through my feelings. When I felt myself buzzing around and off balance, extra effort needed to be made to center back within myself through God and to take time to deal with what was bothering me. I would go off to a quiet place and sit down, resting my head and trying to turn my mind off, letting myself focus and be open to receive God's love.

If I were really wound up, I tried to think of nothing, breathing deeply and calmly, and giving my body a good oxygen supply. I would then gently pray, "God, help me to slow down. Please bring me your peace." The goal is to invite the Holy Spirit deeper within me so that He, not I, can restore peace and give understanding to know what is going on within me. After calming down I often would come to an awareness of what was bothering me.

If I still didn't know what I was feeling, I would probe my memory by asking myself, *Do you feel hurt by some-one? Are you sad? Did what she said hurt you? Did you feel rejected?* At the same time I would mentally scan the inter-actions I had had in the last couple of weeks to see if any given situation seemed to be the culprit. Once identified, the insecurity and anxiety simmered down and my peace was restored.

Sometimes, even after all of this effort, I still could not break through the numbness to discover what I was feeling. Then I tried to journal. I was afraid to do this at first, maybe because once it was on paper I had to face what I was feeling.

I would like to suggest keeping your journal private. I learned this the hard way. Soon after I had left the inpatient portion of the hospital, I went out with some friends. I arrived home six hours later than I had said I would. My poor mom and sister! They were crying, confused and upset when I entered the door. "What's wrong?" I fearfully asked.

"You're six hours late! We thought you had committed suicide!" they replied.

"Where did you get that idea?" I asked, since I was actually doing well and had never mentioned suicide or shown them any signs of wanting to kill myself.

They said, "We read your journal and, well, we were just afraid you had gone and killed yourself!"

I was flabbergasted! Then I recalled that I had recently written, "I just want to kill myself—it is so hard!" It is obvious why they misunderstood that, but I had no intention of killing myself. I had just felt like I wanted to die.

Expressing needs is difficult when one cannot identify with what those needs are. Journaling and talking to others helps us to become aware of our needs so that we can take action. Writing letters to people is also a good way to express ourselves, yet it is always better to talk face to face with people when sharing deep, personal issues, since written letters or emails can always be misunderstood.

Several times, those who received my letters did not interpret them the way that I had intended. I once wrote a 3-paged letter to my mother expressing the details of my years of frustrations. I thought that the letter was mild, fairly clear and not offensive. My motive was to bring issues into the open so that we could grow closer. It was instead very hurtful when she read it, and it took time for us to work through that. Sometimes it is a great idea to write an expressive note, save it for a week, re-read it, and then throw it away.

Even though you may not feel as if you can fully express yourself, I encourage you to gather up your courage to share your thoughts and feelings directly with people, even if you stumble over your words. It will answer the desire of your heart to grow closer to the people in your life. Oftentimes it is only after babbling to a friend that I discover what I am feeling. Take the risk to call someone who will listen. Not only will it help you, but it will also deepen your friendship, trust and love for each other.

Many of the people that I have met who have bulimia are empathetic caretakers of others, and have a great capacity for friendship and love. If we are numb to our deep feelings due to bingeing and purging, we cannot be as loving of a friend as we are capable of being. We are not able to be fully connected to people when we shut down our feelings. We are not being whom God has made us to be if we don't come alive to the full gamete of our emotions.

Loving others and receiving their love is the desire of our hearts, and to do that we must be alive in our feelings. For people who do not have an eating disorder, letting feelings become buried may not be a big deal. But for those with eating disorders, that cannot be afforded. They must be dealt with if freedom from the bondage of bulimia can emerge, and if they want to be fully alive.

Say it Like it Is

I would cringe when someone would look me in the eye and say, "How are you feeling Katie?" A cold chill would run within me, yet with a calm and unaffected face I would reply, "Fine, just great!" I tended to live a double life since I was afraid to show what was I feeling.

I never dared to tell someone, "That hurt me! I feel sad and angry about what you said." Or, "I am just down and lonely today, and I need a hug. Do you want to go out for coffee? I need to talk a bit." It would have been worse to say, "I feel depressed and I feel like I am out of control. I don't know what to do." I was scared to say such things possibly out of fear of how the other person would react. Maybe I would get rejected.

I worried, *What if my sadness caused me to cry in front of someone? I don't know if I could stop. What if my distrust of God and persons in authority over me caused me to go astray, rebel and leave the Church? Heaven-forbid if my anger got so raging that I hit someone!*

I invested a lot of energy into keeping myself safe by suppressing my emotions. It was time to put my energy into a more productive, yet more challenging avenue: learning to express my feelings.

Once I took the lid off some of my feelings, I felt them in extremes. I thought that for the rest of my life I would be an emotional basket case. Many times I wanted to crawl out of my skin rather than continue trying. When I stopped suppressing my emotions, my greatest desire was to curl up in a ball in the corner to soothe my aching heart, mind and body. It was overwhelming—something only those who have gone through it will understand.

When leaving the hospital, I didn't know how I was going to do anything any more. I was absolutely terrified of facing the world as a person awakened to feelings. *How do I act?* I feared whether this new me would be any fun. *Who was this new me anyway?* My feelings were like a roller coaster. Sometimes I sat relaxed, feeling pretty good. Then, the next second, I was spiraling down into the pit of pain and emotional turmoil, all the while fighting off the urge to purge.

Although this stage of recovery seemed as if it would last forever, I knew that the pendulum was bound to swing in the other direction and eventually balance. And it did. God looks with compassion on us and does not judge us as we do ourselves. He knows that one day we will run as long as we keep getting up to try again.

In order to give the burden to Jesus, I needed to *feel* the burden. When I was into the bulimia, I had never felt sad or weighed down from heavy burdens because I would cast my burden onto food. I couldn't cast my burden onto Jesus since I never let myself specifically feel what I needed to cast off!

God knows what we are thinking, so why try to hide from Him? I tended to think, "God is repulsed at me and all I do and with what I am thinking! I can't say what I'm feeling to Him..." Believe me, He has seen and heard much worse and He has not given up on anyone. We can never be bad enough for Him to say, "OK, you've gone too low—I give up on you!" When we come to believe and trust with all of our hearts that we are lovable in our weakest moments, and that He is loving us passionately even when we are in the pits of despair and craziness, this truth will set us free.

What Do You Think?

After I began learning how to express myself, I also started understanding how a person's mind controls his or her feelings. If we think that we are no good and have no talents worth sharing, we will be depressed, self-absorbed, and hate ourselves.

For ages, Scripture has described the battlefield of the mind. Romans 12:2 says, "Do not be conformed to this world, but be transformed by the renewing of your mind, that you may discern the will of God, what is good and pleasing and perfect."

2 Corinthians 10: 3-5 clearly says that the spiritual battle must be fought with God's weapons, "which we use to destroy strongholds. We destroy false arguments; we pull down every proud obstacle that is raised against the knowledge of God; we take every thought captive and make it obey Christ." Now that's battle language! And Jesus said; "the Truth will set you free" (John 8:32).

I didn't have to believe something simply because I felt a certain way. I felt many times as if I wanted to die, but I didn't kill myself. I felt as if I was worthless, but that wasn't the truth. I didn't have to act as if I were worthless. I let the truth guide my actions, not my feelings.

Have any of you sensed a friend's anxiety or slight coldness, and after five seconds of being around them, you are convinced that it is your fault? I have. It has even almost ruined a few relationships, because I was convinced that I knew what my friend was thinking about me. My thoughts led me to feel horrible about myself and to avoid that friend, which then strained our relationship. My negative mind would taunt me with lies that I was a horrible friend, a bore to be around, and a pain in the behind to friends. Ninety-five percent of the time I was right in my perception that something was wrong with my friend that day, but I was often wrong in my interpretation of her feelings.

Often times this judgment of the mind tended to be negative, and more often than not, inaccurate. My head often confirmed what I already believed about myself. I could be correct in my perception but wrong in my conclusions. This self-centered judgment would only leave me ultimately alone, and away from closer relationships to others.

By studying my instruction book, the Bible, along with watching what successful people did, I learned how to maintain myself adequately. God wanted me to change my feelings by changing my rotten thinking. The feelings will follow a healed heart and mind.

Jesus wants us to bring our feelings and thoughts to Him to express them. He is not afraid of them like we are. I always use this type of prayer, and it helps me to bring my problems to God: "Lord, I feel lonely, tired and angry! Now I come to You and give you myself. I bring these feelings to the foot of your cross. I don't know why I am feeling this way, but I ask that You redeem them and show me any wrong thinking that I may have that is behind these feelings. Please now express Yourself in me." Be determined to stick with the prayer until you receive God's peace.

Reprogramming our minds is a tedious, arduous task, particularly for those who have been through years of an addiction, or coupled addictions, in and out of hospitals and counselors. In order to heal our thinking, and learn to express ourselves in all facets of our life, we have to loosen the tight grip we have on our emotions. Once we are more aware of what we are feeling, we can identify more easily with our thinking process that fuels those feelings.

Do You Want to Stop?

Recently, I had the great opportunity of speaking with a high school junior about her struggle with bulimia. We felt like kindred spirits as we shared many similar family and personal experiences.

She, too, had a father who drank "not too much, only like two or three bottles of beer each night and maybe something else," which contributed to the occasions of conflict within her home. She was also involved in sports with a determination to be one of the best. She felt uncomfortable with the whole promiscuous guy-scene and consequently didn't date much. Insecurity and fear were part of her relationships, despite her confident outward appearance. She was very sensitive and often burdened with her sense of responsibility to family and other matters.

I proposed to her that people with bulimia eat to hide feelings stuffed deep within them, but she didn't fully grasp what I meant. When I was in high school, I didn't understand when people tried to talk to me about dealing with my feelings either. *What feelings?* I would silently question. *I'm not feeling anything bad!* I was like a child looking at an aquarium, unable to feel the water and contents of the world inside the glass box. I knew that bingeing and purging weren't normal, but neither was shutting down. At the time I didn't see that the two were related.

The bulimia was expressing on the outside the feelings and pain that I felt inside. As sick as it seemed to others, the bulimia was serving a useful purpose for me. It acted as a filler to secure the gaps in the foundation that seemed to be breaking within and around me. It was a way of feeling in control of my life. As reckless as I may have been, I somehow felt *in control* when I would go on a binge, and when my weight was at a certain number. It was a way of releasing my tension and deeply harbored anger; although I didn't realize that I was tense and angry.

By being sneaky and bingeing on food in our house, I was subtly displaying my anger and fear with all that was happening in my life and family. Perhaps inside I was screaming, *Ha-ha! I can do this and you can't stop me even if you try! Ha! And until you change and make things stable here in the family, I WON'T STOP!* That is one reason why it was hard to stop such a cycle. Even when we have endured decades of bulimia, I think that unresolved feelings from our childhood or adolescence can still motivate us to continue in this destructive behavior.

My high school friend, Kristin, asked me, "There's a part of me that doesn't want to quit bingeing and purging, and I don't know what to do with that. Plus, what's the big deal to do it?" She at least had the courage to be honest, which was something that took me a long time to do. Her bulimia was unconsciously serving a purpose for her. She was determined to see something change within her and around her before she chose to give up the horrible addiction.

In response, I told her, "There's a part of you that doesn't want to stop bingeing and purging because you're getting something out of it. You've got to figure out what that part is and deal with it in a better way. You're right—it does feel good. And you get a sort of a high after a while from bingeing on food and vomiting, and of knowing that no one can make you stop. There is satisfaction and control in it to some extent. It's a way of dealing with our feelings whether we know we have them or not.

"But, Kristin, there are consequences to our bulimia. For example, if I punch this table, whether I admit it or not, the skin and blood cells on my hand will be damaged, some will break, and eventually bruising will show. I can deny that fact and say, 'That didn't hurt', but I can't reverse or stop the natural effects of that punch. There are always consequences to our actions—good and bad—upon our lives."

The sickness of bulimia is that most of us do not mind the bruising and damage to ourselves. In fact, self-destruction can also become an obsession. As the disease progresses, people with bulimia tend to hit a lower and lower bottom. I would even be tempted to secretly compete with other people struggling for a "better bottom". For many, the bottom isn't hit until they totally destroy themselves by death. That drive has to be healed in order to recover.

We who are struggling with an eating disorder know deep down that it isn't normal to eat food and vomit, or to lie about what we are doing to those who ask. Many of us have not stolen food, bled from vomiting, rotted our teeth or incurred heart or organ problems—so the question is raised, "What's the big deal?" That is a great question to ask. Answering it will open for us a whole new dimension and perspective on our lives and futures.

Early on, I also used to tell myself, *I am not doing so badly in school and sports and stuff, so what is the big deal?* At first, the effects are subtle, so it's easy to be blind to the full effects of bulimia. Then, gradually, it gets worse.

By my senior year in High School, although my bulimia was still hidden from most of my family and all but one friend, it was definitely becoming a "big deal". The symptoms of depression and the fact that my volleyball was not improving were evident. I had a hard time fully concentrating. I felt more and more defeated inside and began hating myself because I couldn't stop bingeing and purging. My life was falling apart.

By stuffing in huge quantities of food and then purging, I temporarily kept the volcano from erupting. It gave a sort of adrenaline rush—a "relief" that subdues the turmoil—for a while. Bulimia postpones the inevitable.

For the first few months of the bulimia, bingeing and purging worked quite well and the effects lasted fairly long. Yet the more often I binged and purged, the shorter the benefit became. Eventually I had to do it more often. It wasn't until I totally crashed and burned, ending up in a hospital, that I realized that my bulimia was directly related to long-buried emotions. Even then it took some effort to grasp this emotional reality!

Since that time, I have learned a bit more about feeling. Feelings are meant to be expressed, and not repressed. When emotions get all clogged up, it is harder to reach out for help. We tend to isolate ourselves when we need help the most. Thus, we do not have a safe place to effectively deal with our feelings, except by keeping them buried alive inside. The bulimia then becomes an expression of that inner tension of deep, unresolved issues that we have never faced.

Facing the Truth
Embracing the truth is key to winning the battle. Once

we have begun to unravel the knots of tangled emotions, and have attained a grasp on how to deal with our feelings and thinking, we have to face issues and memories we have been avoiding. If we don't face them head on, they will continue to fuel the fire of an eating disorder. We have to get through this battlefield, because there is no running away if we want to see the ultimate victory.

It was important to begin discovering the roots of my disorder, but at the same time, there were at times more superficial reasons that I was bingeing and purging. My reason for bingeing and purging was sometimes due to being too *h*ungry, *a*ngry, lonely and *t*ired; as the 12 Step Program calls it, *"HALT"*!

Hunger: If we let ourselves go without food for a meal or two, we are most likely setting ourselves up for a binge. Trying to starve myself never worked. When I kept myself hungry, I would usually wind up forking down tons of food before noon. There were other times when I just was not giving my body what it needed. My body would crave a certain nutrient, for example Vitamin C. Instead I would shovel in tons of ice cream out of an effort to quell my body's anxiety. If I had listened to what my body was craving, the binge may have been thwarted.

Anger: The cause of my purging was often suppressed feelings of anger. Perhaps someone had said something hurtful, something did not go my way, or I was mad at myself for some reason. Although I did not typically feel the anger at the moment of the binge and purge, it was fuel for the fire. I will share more about dealing with my anger later in this chapter.

Loneliness: I also had to learn to face my loneliness. Food became my friend, companion, and sole confidant. It was always there to hear my problems. I can not count the number of times I binged and purged because I was longing to be close to someone.

I can dare to say that all persons trapped in the walls of

an eating disorder experience loneliness to some degree. Fear of sharing what was really going on inside troubled me. I thought, *If I share what I'm feeling or thinking with that person, they will get sick of me.* Yet the ache to have a close friend who understood was the cry of my heart. Stifling that God-given desire was easier than facing it. As I began to rely on other people and took more risks in relationships, food became less of a priority and less of a drive.

Lastly, HALT stands for being tired. Tired of bingeing. Tired of hiding. Tired of lying. Tired of wasting money, time and energy. If I had had a big binge in the morning, I would often fall into bingeing in the evening simply because I was tired of resisting temptations. To silence the barrage of thoughts, I gave in to bingeing and purging.

And so I used to use HALT as a way to examine my conscience when I felt like going on a binge. *Katie, are you hungry or angry at something? Are you lonely or tired?* Sometimes those provoking questions then led me to probe even deeper and discover some of the roots that were the significant sources of fueling my bulimia.

Pulling out the Roots

I discovered many roots that fed my disorder. One root that perpetuated my eating disorder was a fear of emotional pain. By avoiding any encounter that could potentially cause an uncomfortable feeling, I lived in a constant state of anxiety, always interiorly running. I wasn't at home within myself, so I lost touch with who I am. As I result, I built walls that kept me from living my life with love and freedom, which distorted my personality.

Flowing from this distortion of my personality, self-destructive and negative thoughts caused me to be more awkward and anxious around other people. Increasing degrees of indecision, shame, and feelings of being lost replaced any solid foundation I may have had before the eating disorder started. I was, in a sense, homeless and rest-less, looking for something or someone to fill me.

The twelve steps of Alcoholics Anonymous gave me a helpful approach to address these roots that needed to be healed. They have a saying called the three A's: *Awareness*, *Acceptance* and *Action*. The first step is in admitting that damage has been done both from others, and to others. We become aware of what the problem is. Tragedy and pain touch all of our lives. No person can escape it, as hard as they may try. We can never conceal our sorrow, sadness and gnawing aches with external distractions. They will never disappear as we so desperately hope. We inevitably have to face everything and everyone that we are running from.

I was the queen of trying to skip this crucial first step, particularly of admitting the pain that other people had caused me. It was my forte. I would defend the person who hurt me, saying, "He is a great person, so kind and help-ful...it didn't bother me that much but there were some things he did that kind of, well, sort of, a little bit hurt me. But I'm O.K. now."

I was afraid of experiencing the pain associated with bringing up the memories of the ways in which I felt hurt. As irrational as it may sound, I was afraid that by re-experi-encing them, I would hurt those people more. I felt as if I had hurt them enough and I did not want to do that any more. I was afraid that somehow what I said would damage our relationship further.

For example, I was afraid that if I let myself feel sad, disappointed and angry that my sister was not always supportive of me while growing up, expressing it now would hurt her. I figured that if she knew how she had hurt me, she would feel terrible, and might not want to be close to me again. She might even get upset and not talk to me any more. It was scary to let myself feel such things. I was already feel-ing horrible and vulnerable inside, and particularly needy for sisterly support, so such conclusions seem very plausible.

When my sister realized some of her shortcomings, she did feel horrible. And I did feel terrible that she felt that way. But this is all a necessary element of going through such things, and we grew closer as a result.

I finally was able to work through my feelings and become aware of how I felt about our relationship growing up, as well as in the present. That enabled me to go to the second stage that AA outlines: *Acceptance*. This calls for a trusting surrender to accept the circumstances, and the fact that without some intervention they will remain this way. Once we accept such things, and stop pretending that they are not true, we are free to make necessary changes, and God is freer to do what He needs to do.

By being honest with how I felt hurt, I had the courage to face the sins that I had committed against her. I was certainly not innocent in our relationship. I had to take responsibility for the selfish ways in which I had responded to her episodes of coldness, and for the other things that I had done. As I chose to break down the walls I had built up—walls that prevented me from loving her—my heart was changed. I was able to truly forgive her and to forgive myself.

The last step was *Action*. This step came in to play as I made choices to change the way I related to my sister. It resulted in both of us being free to love each other more. There are no longer skeletons in the closet and we are much closer because I was able to work through my pain and move on to forgiveness and pursuing a closer bond with her.

After I worked through my relationship with my big sister, it forced me to look at how I treated my little sister. In so many ways I was not there for her and didn't look out for her. As I faced the deep pain of my own selfishness and coldness through the years growing up, I was free to repent to her, God and myself. As a result she and I are becoming closer. It has helped me to become more comfortable with repenting for how I have hurt others!

Headway was made when I gathered up courage and admitted the specific damage that was done to me by other persons, without having to protect them. Most of the time the person's actions were unintentional, or they were merely acting out of their own woundedness, but they still hurt my heart. It was painful to admit my hurts, but it eventually freed me to love the person more deeply and to reach the goal I longed for: closeness and connection with others.

My hunger was also for intimate relationships. First with myself; to know and love the woman God created me to be. I also longed to see and create beauty both on the inside and out. I wanted to be an instrument in making a difference in people's lives; to be accepted, appreciated and known by others, God and myself. But it all seemed so out of reach considering the complexity of my eating disorder.

Uncovering these feelings and deep desires allowed me to look for ways to deal with them and fulfill them in a healthy way. I was starving to be deeply loved in a more intimate way. For so long, I was never in touch with this beautiful desire. I was afraid to face it. *What if I opened myself up to the desire to be loved and then someone I trusted rejected me or used me? What if I let myself be vulnerable to someone in an effort to build them up, and they stabbed me in the back?* I thought. It was easier to never risk anything and to keep my safe boundaries.

As I slowly began penetrating those self-made walls, I found an increasing joy and release in my soul, and the bulimia symptoms began to lessen.

Along with my longing for deeper relationship with other people was a gnawing desire to be close to God. Did I really know God? Was the concept I had of Him real or distorted? If I truly believed that God was distant and displeased with the core of me, then I could never love others or myself fully and passionately. I came to see my sins and bulimia as tumors that had grown on good flesh - they were distortions of something good. The Great Physician had to do surgery.

I trusted that when I came to know the real character of God, I would not be afraid to be close to Him. There is no reason to fear true love.

Too many times we become hardhearted because we have been hurt. We close ourselves off from loving our family and friends. We feel justified to stay angry with them and, if we are honest, even to hate them. "They don't love me the way I need to be loved! So why should I make more of an effort to reach out to them?" It is understandable in some situations, but if we are closed to the possibility and responsibility of loving them with all of our hearts, as Christ empowers us to love, we will not be free. We are made to love. When we refuse to do this we subtly destroy ourselves.

I find many people hesitant to call a sin a sin for fear of falling into self-condemnation. But if we are honest about our woundedness and are sad for the negative impact that our sins have had on other people, ourselves and our relationships with God, it will help us to hate our bad behavior and want to receive the grace to change for the better. Once confessed, we can let it go and forget it as He does and be healed of whatever is weighing us down. We can not let go of something that we have never embraced. We must first feel it and accept that that is part of us. Then we will see change happen.

Once we have moved through the steps of awareness and acceptance, and are living the action step, we can choose to be thankful for every situation. 1 Thessalonians 5:18 says, "In all circumstances, give thanks, for this is the will of God for you in Christ Jesus." When I dared to take the seemingly preposterous challenge of thanking God for hard things like being disappointed, hurt, losing something or doing something without thinking, I was somehow released to rise above the difficult feelings. When I began applying His Scriptural teaching that we must be thankful in everything, difficult situations were utterly transformed. Give thanks for feeling so awful? Yes!

I would say, *Thank you, Jesus that I feel so insecure and jittery right now. Thank you!* After many times of using the "faking it till I make it" technique, I began believing what I was saying. I said, *Yea—thanks Lord that I am feeling this way. I know you are in control and feelings are only feelings. Just because I feel out of control, doesn't mean that I am, or that You are not in control. I guess You are teaching me something through this. Thanks a lot!*

Facing all of those difficult feelings and sins is extremely challenging, but the more frequently we face them, the easier it is to do so. As it becomes more natural to face ugly aspects about ourselves, we do not have to hide as we have for so long. Admitting this frees us to be more ourselves and to share with others.

For a long time I thought that if I could just stop bingeing and purging, then my nightmare would be over. For many years I wrestled with my will to try to make myself stop. Then I learned that merely controlling my food intake would not solve the problem. I had to deal with the roots that were fueling the addiction. If I didn't deal with the roots of my addiction, I would never be set free. I had to make a commitment to receive healing for the brokenness inside.

May the Lord continue to strengthen you and keep you open to see what you need to see. May you grow in the grace of awareness of who you are, acceptance of yourself and others, and the wisdom to do what is necessary to receive the freedom He desires for you.

CHAPTER FOUR

Caught in Anger

I still chuckle as I remember when I told my hospital counselor, "I don't have any anger. I'm not an angry person." Well, let me tell you, I've discovered that I have a deep passionate ability to be angry that I never knew existed! It was actually one of the roots of my disorder.

Everyone struggles with anger to some degree or another. Although I did not realize it at the time, my bulimia was often an attempt to expel the anger and rage I had built up within. There came a point soon after I graduated from Franciscan University, when I knew I had to face the mountain of anger I felt inside. I was afraid that if I let the cap off, I would begin hitting and screaming at people and throwing uncontrolled tantrums in the middle of the room. That's what it felt like.

As I slowly unscrewed the cap of my repressed anger, it was at times expressed inappropriately and I unintentionally hurt those around me. But in time the pendulum swung to the middle.

Depression is a symptom of hidden anger, along with other suppressed feelings. If I had the opportunity to be diagnosed, I am sure that I would have been classified as depressed during the course of my recovery. When the symptoms of depression last over weeks and inhibit our growth, then it is a concern and possibly needs medication. Yet for me, the depression was spurring me on to delve deeper into the roots of my illness.

It was necessary for me to go through that stage of feeling down in the dumps. To feel and admit that I was depressed, and to be okay with being so down, was great progress for me. For a long time I had expected myself to be Super-Kate: to never feel down, to have a smile for everyone I met, and to feel ashamed for even feeling a moment of depression. That had to change.

I had to examine if I was angry and unforgiving toward God because the root of sin is the suspicion that God is not really as good as He says He is. And certainly I didn't fully trust Him to be always good. Unforgivenness and a need for healing can be masked by anger. When we become hurt in a relationship, or where abuse occurred it is easy to stay angry, resentful and disappointed, including our relationship with God.

I was stuck there for a while. I felt as if it was my right to blame a person for the way I was feeling and the damage I was left to work through. It was as if I wanted to punish that person and attain justice.

Those are all normal feelings and good to admit. Not admitting them will block us from moving on. But there is more to it than just admitting those feelings. We need to receive healing from the damaged emotions, and then choose to forgive.

Forgiveness is key. When the inner wounds are exposed and healed by grace, forgiveness can naturally flow. The true sign that your heart has been healed in a relationship is that the anger has moved to forgiveness, and ultimately to desire to spiritually bless the person who hurt you. And that's so hard!

Now, when I feel angry, I ask myself a few questions: Is my anger acting as a shield of self-protection against any perceived or real pain, sorrow or sadness that I am feeling? Or is it a healthy reaction to something unjust that has happened? Have I fallen into pouting? I do not have to be vulnerable if I keep the wall of anger up, and I can stay safe within my barrier. Dealing with my anger was another key to experiencing freedom, and I knew that I could depend on God's grace and leading me to get me through.

Humiliations

I learned more about how to express my emotions and discover the roots by attending support group meetings. The meetings that I attended gave me comfort because they showed me that there were others who struggled, and that we shared similar stories. Sharing what I went through with other people who understood dissipated some of the shame and humiliation that plagued me.

It is amazing what lengths we can go to in order to hide our addictions. I memorized which public toilets would flush because it was a panicky feeling to have a toilet not completely flush after I vomited. This happened on a number of occasions.

When it did happen, I would usually wait until no one was in the restroom, and then leave quickly so that the next person would never know it was me who made the mess. On a few occasions, I was in a private home and had to fish the vomit out and dispose of it in the trash or sink, praying that they would not notice the bits left in the bowl. How humiliating and degrading that was! It compounded shame upon shame.

One of the most humiliating times in my life was when I was caught bingeing at a Southern California supermarket. The ironic thing was that I happened to be on my way to a

Twelve-Step Bulimic/Anorexic Anonymous meeting when the familiar irresistible urge to binge and purge hit me.

I stopped at a market five minutes away from the meeting place. I walked down the isles, inconspicuously eating food from the bins in the bulk food section: something I had done so many times before. After eating a bunch of cookies and two muffins I left the empty bags on a shelf and went to purchase $1.50 worth of food so I wouldn't look so obvious leaving the store without buying something. I was also appeasing my guilt of eating the store's food without paying for it.

I was once again filled with shame as I walked to my car, eager to get to my meeting. Amidst being preoccupied with planning where to vomit, I was suddenly startled by the two men behind me calling, "Ma'am! Ma'am, excuse me!" I turned around to find two well built men dressed casually who quickly approached me and took me by the arm saying, "We saw you take and eat the food in the store without paying. You will need to come with us." I was shocked! Is this really happening? I was in a fog.

They walked me through the store into a back room where there was another man: clearly the boss. They were somewhat rough and frustrated with me saying, "Do you know what you did is a public offense and you should be taken to jail for this? You should at least get a $500 fine for stealing food!" At that point I didn't even care. I knew I deserved this prosecution. I also knew how I hated myself when I was doing it, and that it wasn't the real "me" that did it at all.

The men went on to ask, "Why did you do it, did you not have money?" With deep feelings of self-disgust I softly said, "No, I have money."

Frustrated, they said, "Then why did you do it?" Tears welled up in my eyes. I knew I stole food in part to make me hate myself more. I shamefully explained that I had bulimia and that I was on my way to a meeting. I told them I would never steal food again.

They said, "We will let you go this time, but if you ever return to this store and we find you stealing again, we will prosecute you!" They then released me. I felt like the scum of the earth as I was escorted out of the store, vowing to myself to never to steal again. Although it didn't stop me from subsequent binges, I kept that commitment.

I felt so bad about myself that I saw the degrading acts of purging and bingeing as a sort of justice needing to be imparted upon my already wounded self. I cringe at such memories of what I did simply because I would never do it now, but I understand I did it because I was trapped in a viscous self-destructive cycle that was impossible to break alone.

The Awful Path of Self-Destruction

We all know the potential side-effects of an eating disorder. Some people with bulimia have unfortunately damaged their teeth and esophagus from the constant acid, and their intestinal track from laxatives. Some people's hearts have been affected from the electrolyte imbalance, which has landed them in the hospital. Most everyone's concentration and rational thought processes are often severely impaired. And there are some, God rest their souls, who aren't alive to share their story.

We can't forget the pain endured by family members and friends who watch us go through this and live with the pain that they can't fix us and make things better. There is no escaping the issue of suffering when dealing with an eating disorder.

Even though I didn't incur any known physical effects from the bulimic actions, I fell into my own vices of self-harm. After I had ceased the almost ten years of purging, a new wave of feelings came to the surface that I had never felt before. Everything within me wanted to avoid the deep anger towards others, the gut wrenching sorrow, neediness, the passionate sexual attraction to men, longing for solid friendships, the homesickness and jealousy. I felt crazy in this uncharted territory of the land of feelings.

I was working through a lot of tough issues with my counselor, and as a result I felt as if I was bouncing off the walls. I was too afraid to express my neediness for a hug, to talk, or to cry with someone. At times I wanted to scream inside, and to run away from the "me" I now was getting to know; but there was nowhere to run. Eating food and not purging didn't give me the same high that I had when I did purge. Instead, I turned my volcanic passions inward and began to take my self-hate out in a new way.

I was upset for a number of reasons. My volleyball playing went sour, I had trouble confiding in friends, my relationship with my parents was strained, and my dad had been a drinker. I was angry with men's vulgarity, too, and felt uncomfortable about my femininity. I felt like a little kid inside at times. I wanted the love and support of older people, and I was angry that I didn't have it. Deep down I just wanted to be held, like a mother holds their child, and I was ashamed and hated myself that I had such desires. My anger also masked the deep fear of who I was becoming.

I wanted to escape all of this pain. I found a new vice, a new addiction to avoid the inner hurt. The physical scars on my arms, legs and abdomen will forever silently tell the story. It, like the bulimia, worked for a short time to "relieve" myself from the inner pain, but in the long run, only caused many more problems. Any suicidal thoughts were motivations to experience peace within because I couldn't live inside myself any longer.

Instead of feeling the pain of possible rejection from a peer, I would inflict physical harm upon myself. It seemed easier to hurt myself physically than to face the reality that sometimes friends hurt us and we hurt them.

Somehow, in a sick way, it felt good to hurt myself, because I was reinforcing the lies that I believed about myself. Katie, you are bad within the core of you! Those you love are disappointed in you and are tired of you! You're different from everyone! But this was only another vice, like bulimia, that kept my guard up so as to shut myself off from those I wanted to love and who wanted to love me.

I began to see that there was no limit or end to my addictive self-destruction when I imagined myself cutting off a limb, and still not being satisfied with the degree of self-harm. At this point I realized that I was really sick, so I began taking the steps to face some of the pain I was running from. If I didn't face myself and walk through the feelings, I would eventually destroy my life. It is a horrible feeling to go though recovery. At low points it feels like death is a better option.

Just as a child learns best if the parent provides a loving environment and positive feedback, so recovery will speed up as we learn to treat ourselves with dignity and respect, as God intends for us to be cared for.

Please allow me to pray with you:

> Dear Lord, I pray that You protects us. God, help us to reach out and ask for that support from others and from You. Take away our shame and let us see ourselves with love and compassion as You do. Let these scars of ours be washed away by Your healing love. We are so needy of Your love, oh Lord... Embrace us now, Father. Amen.

CHAPTER FIVE

A Surrender to Love

Do you know why God chose to create you? You were created because your Father in heaven didn't have one like you and wanted one as beautiful and unique as you are. God loves you so much that He wants you to enjoy an amazing relationship with Him. There is such joy when we are able to *really* believe that we are entirely loved by God.

The solid foundation of our healing must stand on an understanding God's loving heart for us. Then the healing of our shame and inner wounds can be accomplished. I couldn't dare look at my deepest fears and secrets until I began to receive unconditional love from someone who knew me inside and out. God was the one I needed.

When I began trying to understand who God is, I inevitably came face to face with a paradox: If God is all good and loving, why do bad things happen to me and other people? I lived with unanswered questions as to why He didn't stop this or that from happening, or why I had to go through certain things.

I would raise my hands in praise as I sang songs about God's great love for me, but if I was honest, my heart was cold and even angry at the proposition that God really loves me, or that He is *really* good. Many of us are afraid to be that honest about any doubts.

If I can't be comfortable to approach God and to receive from Him, I can't get fully healed. When we do not confront these doubts about the sincerity of God's love, it's possible build a cloud of unbelief.

Why is it so hard for us to trust God and to be convinced that He is madly in love with us? I believe the reason is because we often doubt that God is as good as He says He is thus we refuse to fully trust Him. Some of us fear that God may act like other authority figures have in their past and mistreat them. Other of us fear that trusting God will lead us to a suffering that cannot be handled. We conclude, "God doesn't have a heart of compassion because I cry out and He doesn't change me!" Or "he's passive. He loves me but He isn't powerful enough to help me." Believing this, many of us run from Him and act like we don't hear His invitation to draw near to Him and trust him with our lives.

Maybe some of you have seen the 90's movie, "A Man Without a Face", with Mel Gibson. I think it's an excellent movie. The whole town was afraid of him and made him up to be such a horrible, evil man, both because of his past accusations of sexual abuse and because of his terribly scarred face from an accident. People would physically distance themselves from him, except for one little boy who dared to get to know this "monster", as some people called him. The two got to be great friends. Certainly this boy didn't buy into what others perceived this man to be because he saw something wonderful through the scars—a beautiful face.

Like this story, sometimes we are stuck in a wrong perception of God. We then keep ourselves at a distance for fear of getting hurt in some unknown way. If we dare to move forward like this little boy, there are many beautiful surprises behind the mask that we sometimes put on God.

I had always thought that I trusted God and on one level, I did. But I came to a certain low point after I left the hospital in 1987 when I doubted whether I really trusted anyone, let alone God. It was a terrifying state to be in.

Every time I went to read the scriptures it would incite guilt and fear because I would read stories about God commanding people to kill others because of their wickedness. Such harsh Old Testament passages only left me feeling like I was the next person to be slain. His justice was too extreme for me to comprehend and I felt like God was harshly judging my every move.

I was so hard on myself and so I believed God treated me the same way. And *if* God was who I perceived Him to be, it was appropriate to be afraid and distrustful of Him! It would be wise to put up a guard against someone who loves you one moment and then is ready to throw you to the lions the next, simply out of spite. Although I felt that way toward God, it wasn't who God really was. I needed to know who God *really* was so that I could put my trust in the truth and not force myself to be vulnerable to a make-believe concept God. Only then would I be able to really trust God, others and myself.

Within that faulty conception of God, I couldn't grasp my call to be holy. My perfectionism and harshness on myself made pursuit of holiness seem like a stepladder to heaven, an earning of God's love for me. Because of a somewhat legalistic relationship with God, I perceived a part of Him as a harsh, impatient Master who demanded perfection from me his servant, yet all under the disguise of being a loving God. I assumed He expected me to be perfect and was mad when I made a mistake. Often times authority figures in our own lives ingrained such an image, which we then imposed upon the ultimate authority in our life.

Yet, God can separate the "sin" from "Katie". He sees my potential and is supplying me with all the grace needed to continue on that journey of wholeness and holiness. It takes time; and He knows that. I'm the one that is impatient. If He really wasn't happy with us at this moment, I think He would hurry up the process of our conversion and recovery and "zap" us, and quickly shape us into a holy state.

Instead, He loves and accepts me enough to call me to a higher place. I had to be committed to knowing the real character of God in order to be healed so that I didn't unknowingly react out of a misconstrued fear of God and then distance myself from Him, simply because of a false perception of Him.

The Awesome Love of God

True love heals. Every human longs to possess it and to be possessed by it. God looks at each of us with such tender eyes, beckoning us to come closer to Him and accept His love. His passion never fades away no matter what we do. *This* incredible love makes me *want* to change for the better!

Toward the end of my recovery when I was having a hard time understanding God's love, I journaled this:

> God, I feel so numb, I have no desire to even be close with You or others. I don't even feel compassion for myself. I am concerned because I am feeling unconcerned. I cannot change; I need your touch Almighty God. The spiral of discouragement and mediocrity are surging downward and I'm like a leaf on a stream. I wish that I was a star, a brilliant daughter doing feats of wonder, and yet You are satisfied with my lowly state, more satisfied than if I was a brilliant star. Why?
>
> No, I have found You to be amazingly gentle, yet at the same time fierce. Fierce enough to let me, whom You love, become

weak so that You can teach me Your strength
and to allow my own strength rise from this
lump of clay. I am finding that as You allow
me to endure the fires of these trials and then
I become stronger than ever. I learn things I
would never have learned without this grace.
No I don't understand Your ways, Lord, You
often seem very strange to me but I guess it's
because Your ways aren't mine.

This is what I love so much about my God—that I can
let it all hang out and not pretend to be someone I'm not. No
matter how weak, depressed or how out of control I may be
and no matter how far I may stray from God, He never
changes and is always there to help me. Whenever I accept
His help and grace in an open honest way, I am saved again
and again, and I can love God through the whole process.

We just need to keep hanging in there and not give up
when we feel humiliated. And sometimes, just "hanging" is
about all we can do since we are so broken and wounded
inside. Even if you give up, there is a second, third,
fourth...and 70 x 7th chance! He *never* gives up on you.
There is no amount of bingeing and purging you could do
that would disgust Him enough to send you away. He loves
you! Open your eyes to see the Truth! Even if *you* deny this
reality, it will still be true and His presence will still be waiting for you. He will *never* give up on you, even when you
give up on yourself.

Being depressed and plunged into a pit is one of the
most precious opportunities to grow in our love for God. For
then we can say, "God, I want to offer myself to you in this
horrible spot I am in and let you do with me as You desire".
That is the sweetest surrender and sign of our love for God.
He is so pleased with that!

Wherever we are at, we can all use a deeper touch of

God. Let us invite the Holy Spirit to fan our flames. If your flame is only a burnt out wick, even crumbling when you go to light it—*Have hope!!!* Maybe parts of you are still very empty because you've been hurting inside so badly for so long. Maybe you're afraid of becoming too radical for God, or maybe you are so worn down and discouraged from years of struggle that you don't have any energy to get up and do anything.

Whatever your fears are, I encourage you to open your heart to the Holy Spirit's healing work in you, even if it's just a minuscule, unfeeling prayer. *God loves you!*

I Surrender!

After about years of bulimia and an infinite amount of attempts to stop it, I finally admitted more deeply than I had ever before that I was *not* in control of stopping this addiction. I always knew I needed help, but I never admitted from the depths of my soul that I was not ultimately in control. Fear of surrendering had plagued me for so many years.

How obvious could it be that I was out of control when I lost my volleyball scholarship, went into a hospital for six weeks, lived in a halfway house for five months, and got confronted by the police for stealing food during a binge? Yet I not only had to admit it in my head, but I also had to believe it within the deepest recesses of my heart, mind and soul that I was powerless. It was scary to admit because it left me feeling so desperately out of control. There had been nothing in my life I had set out to do that I hadn't accomplished; this was the first. "In my weakness He is strong" is what I have learned to proclaim (II Corinthians 12:9).

During most of my illness, I would depend on myself and say, *OK, Lord, help me try harder and keep my commitments. I know You expect me to overcome this and I don't want to let You down.* Often, even before finishing that thought, I would be off running to do another binge.

I was unclear what that element was that He was to do, and still am not clear, but without that part, I was helpless to fully overcome. Certainly there were many things I had to do including facing my fears and stepping out to share my feelings with others, but as for relieving me of that nagging drive to binge and purge—He had to do it. I proved I couldn't.

One day, I sat down and prayed,

> God, You know I have been trying with all of my heart to quit this. I really don't want to be doing this, although it may seem I do. Trying to overcome this is the hardest thing I've ever done. You know if it were in my power, this second I would stop this horrible thing and eat right. But I can't and I am sorry for that. Yet, for some strange reason, I think You want me to admit that I can't. Are You mad? Do You like to see people like me struggle? No, You're not like that.

> I believe You want to show me a new way, a way where You carry me through somehow. You're letting me learn the hard way so that I really learn how to depend on you well. I'd like to figure out how You do it, but I guess that's not for me to know. But I admit, Lord, that if You don't intervene and do a miracle to change me and relieve me of this bondage, I will be 80 years old and still struggling with bingeing and purging.

> I believe You love me so much that You will take this obsession away in Your perfect timing. Only <u>You</u> can. You know I've tried! I

hope You do it as soon as possible, but I will wait. That's all I can do.

And if I continue today and tomorrow to binge and purge, then so be it. I will not feel overly guilty like I have been feeling for so long. I will not beat myself up, but comfort myself and love myself through this, knowing all I can do is to wait for Your mercy and healing. Lord, thanks for what you will do in me!

This was a breakthrough prayer for me and although the next day I did binge and purge, as I stuffed the food down by the handful I reflected on what I had prayed the day before and felt a strange peace and joy welling up within my heart. I *know* my Father hears every prayer and answers them according to what's best for me.

Things didn't exactly change after that moment, but I began trusting God in a deeper way after that day. I had sincerely surrendered from my gut and I was willing then to wait for God to fill in the cracks of recovery. I knew that He would stick with me through it all and not give up on me.

I have been able to apply this principle of surrendering to many areas of my life. For example food, pride, bad attitudes, fears, or self-protection, whatever area it is, I can come to God confidently to experience freedom.

Let me offer the following analogy to explain my picture of surrendering. Picture two puzzle pieces. There is one large piece that has a small, jagged piece missing in the middle. The large piece symbolizes God's part in recovery. Our piece is a jagged piece that needs to be meticulously cut to fit inside that larger piece. God knows what the piece is to look like and offers direction and grace to form it, but we have to take the initiative to go through the processes of formation.

Thus we go through a lot of hard times, inner healing,

facing things that are difficult and learning more about God and ourselves; while at he same time, our puzzle piece shape is constantly being remolded into the right shape.

Although this whole process of transformation is important, there is one point when the lights go on and that puzzle piece snaps into place. *Oh! This is what God means by surrendering and walking by the Spirit!* says the jagged puzzle piece that now fits so nicely in the big picture. Really it's the bigger puzzle piece that makes up most of the picture but because the smaller piece is being molded, it feels like it's the main picture and most important piece.

Many of us who are struggling amidst an addiction in which we blow it several times a day, and everyday for years, begin to doubt whether God will stick with us and endure this long process of making our puzzle piece fit into His. I tell you, He will! Don't give up hope! The following stories of these women declare this hope.

A Woman in Love

God can restore what has been destroyed and damaged by our sins and heal the damage others have done to us. Even if you have been in and out of hospitals most of your life, you can't hold a job because of constant suicidal thoughts and you feel like no one cares. Someone cares. Not only that, but He died for you so that you could be free. Being loved doesn't mean the road to recovery will be free of pain, but hang on to Jesus' end of His coat and let Him bring you to higher ground. He wants you to know He is with you through every step. He cares more than you can even imagine.

God wants to be so close to you. But He can't fix everything, unless permission is given. He is a gentleman and He needs your surrender like Mary, Jesus' mother did, "Behold, I am the handmaiden of the Lord, be it done unto me according to Your word." (Luke 1:38)

It is your decision to keep those doors of hope open. Hope is a choice. I believe the only reason you will close the doors of hope is if you believe the lie that you are so bad that not even the God will endure you. But believing this lie will allow despair to set in. It's a form of false pride for then you are greater than Gods plan for your life.

But as Mother Teresa said, "God desires faithfulness, not success." I kept trying to work through recovery even though I was caught up in sin and weakness. I kept choosing to hope. He certainly did not reward me because of my success or strength, because that was obviously lacking!

So, we can surrender to the Lord in confidence that He will respect us and treasure our willing submission. The road to recovery is not easy since we need to be struck down in areas that our insecurities and fears have been built up. It seems to me that we sometimes need to be torn and humiliated in order to break our wounded heart. Once broken, we can fully heal.

Surrendering is likened to a child whose leg was once broken but never set in a cast. It most probably will heal on its own, but will heal inadequately so that the child can't run fast, or possibly even walk well. In order to fix it properly, the parent must let the doctor re-break it. That causes a lot of pain, maybe even more than did the original accident. Then the leg is put in a cast for several weeks until the bone heals rightly, which takes time and sacrifice from the child since she has to be laid up for so long.

That child and parent could, if they wanted, never deal with the handicap and go through life with the limp and they would most probably cope adequately. Yet this child, who would one day be an adult, would never know what it was like to be free of the limp or experience the exhilaration of being able to run and play. This person could not live life to its fullest potential.

It's the same with us. Will we be willing to risk letting

ourselves be hurt again in order to heal? The path is not easy, but He has promised to help us. Yet He cannot take away all the pain that needs to be endured in order to heal; nevertheless, I've found that the pain somehow makes the growth and healing more permanent and beautiful.

I've Got Family!

Have you ever sat and pondered the fact that God was a little eight-pound helpless crying baby? How much more vulnerable can you get than that? I would have never dreamed up such a thing in my wildest imaginations. I don't even think Hollywood could have come up with such an incredible story.

Then, as if that weren't enough to show us how much He wants to parent us, His Son Jesus is sent. He grows up and suffers a most cruel death by crucifixion on a cross in order to make a way for us to be healed and to come home. All of God's efforts to reach out to us are about bringing us back to our Father's home so that we can be family again. He longs to be in communion with us and to have our friendship! It is His nature to desire this so intently for that's what Love compels.

Many of us have a hard time with accepting God as a Father, and may even avoid calling Him that. In my life, working through my father issues has been a significant key to my recovery. There were many episodes where I experienced healing of my relationship with God as Father, but one time stands out.

A few years ago, every time the subject of "fathers" came up, I felt an anxiety in my heart and I didn't know what was causing it. Various incidences were bringing to light the fact that I was still feeling resistant to letting God get closer to me, and I to my "Abba Daddy". In other people's eyes I had a good relationship with God, but I knew there was something holding me back from going deeper.

Even though I prayed to go deeper, my heart was closed.

After a few months of growing more uncomfortable because I knew I was avoiding something, I dug a bit deeper to see what was really going on inside. Why was He not answering my prayer? Was *I* was the obstacle in the answer to this prayer?

Finally after talking to a friend I realized I wasn't being honest with myself. The truth was that I didn't even *want* to be more intimate—I was afraid. I was at a safe place and didn't want to budge. I already was feeling very exposed and vulnerable in my everyday life due to a lot of changes happening and going to and from mission work, that I didn't want more intimacy with my Father because that meant I had to get more vulnerable.

I knew I had to make a choice: Would I stay stagnant or face this challenge of letting God heal me of any blocks that remained in my relationship with Him as Father? If I said no, I had to face the effect of an increasing apathy and numbness, along with a draining of whatever remaining passion I was feeling for relationship with others and God.

After a long inner struggle, I made the choice to take a step deeper. I got really honest with myself and with God and told Him how weak and tired I felt, and how my heart was hurting over a number of issues; I told Him how I was homesick, lonely and afraid. I asked Him to meet me where I was and to help me get through this.

As I sat quietly in my room that night and I looked deeper as to what was holding me back from experiencing more intimacy with God and others. As I waited in silence, I began to see deep fear inside my heart and how I was afraid to get physically and emotionally close to a father. I began recognizing the blocks I felt toward my own dad.

For so long I tried to carry my family's burdens and my dad's difficulties. I felt responsible to bring peace to my family. I was also uncomfortable with my femininity, which in turn made it more difficult to receive nurturing from my dad during my teen years. In addition, I had a fear that a father wouldn't actively protect me against verbal or physical harm from others. I lay on my bed that night emotionally drained.

I then was quite aware that I had projected these feelings of fear onto my relationship with my heavenly Dad. I couldn't seem to separate the two. In whatever way I perceived my own dad, was how I was feeling toward my heavenly dad.

Knowing that my God would surely answer my prayers, I confidently asked Him to help me to trust Him and to separate the feelings of my own dad, and Him. I wanted Him to replace any remaining fear I held in my heart toward Him as Father. Once I was able to make that distinction, I felt Him speak to my heart from Isaiah 54 about his deep and tender love for me and His promises for peace.

I sobbed and let the tears wash me of any hurt, disappointment and anger that needed to be cleansed. In my room that night, I declared my forgiveness for my own dad, for the areas that he was not reflecting God's Fatherly character, and asked God to bless him abundantly.

Maybe you can't hold a job or handle school because your eating disorder has messed your mind and body up so much. Whatever you're going through, you are lovable—absolutely, unconditionally lovable. We cannot earn any love; it is a mystery we can only surrender to and believe in faith. Our hope must be that God's grace and mercy will carry us through. And He will, just hang in there.

CHAPTER SIX

Healing the Shame

For you who have never had bulimia, if you want to know what that next urge to binge and purge feels like, imagine a huge twelve-foot California wave, just about to crash on you and your board. Or imagine being on a one-lane road with a semi-truck coming toward you. It seems unstoppable. So many times I silently shrieked, *Oh no! It's back...Here I go again. I hate this!*

Confronting and healing the shame in my life was a key factor in helping me stop these crashing waves. Dr. Dan Allender, the author of <u>The Wounded Heart Workbook</u> defines shame. "Shame is the horrible feeling that we are seen as deficient and undesirable by someone who we hope will deeply enjoy us. It starts when someone whose opinion matters to us find out one of our dark secrets, and we are exposed...As fallen humans, our natural response to the fear of exposure is hiding—denial and deception." (P. 55)

I would convince myself, because of my fear of looking weak in front of others, *I can handle this temptation. I have it under control. I don't need to call a friend or leave this room full of food. I've been abstinent for so long that know I won't give into the temptation.* Thinking I could go it alone was like playing with hot coals. The drive toward bulimia weakened once I began really working on the roots of bulimia which included my shame-based longings and desires.

Shame is a normal human emotion, and if experienced in the right manner, it can keep us within healthy boundaries and even stimulate personal growth. For example if you purposely did something to offend your friend, you would feel shame. If you pay attention to that shame and then apologize, it can mature you and heal your relationship.

All too often, those who have been caught in an addiction know shame in it's unproductive extreme. John Bradshaw, author of Healing the Shame that Binds You says, "Food addictions are clear syndromes of toxic shame...Shame as a healthy emotion can be transformed into shame as a state of being. As a state of being, shame takes over one's whole identity. To have shame as an identity is to believe that one's being is flawed, that one is defective as a human being. Once shame is transformed into an identity, it becomes toxic and dehumanizing" (p. 97, vii).

I believe that toxic *shame*—shame as a state of being— is the culprit that often perpetuated many episodes of my eating disorder. By falling into a cycle of addiction, shame just feeds upon itself, heaping coals upon coals and pricks away at the hope for recovery. Often times I felt horribly shameful for wanting to be close to someone or worse yet to be held; or of feeling insecure about myself or empty inside—this is when I would turn to bingeing and purging to wash myself of that feeling. The food regime intensified my shame and self-disgust. Then I could be distracted from other inner issues by focusing on the shame and self disgust.

Once I realized the significant role that shame played in my life, I knew I had to get to the root of it. I began tracing the lines of my deep, paralyzing fear and shame, like one would do with a knotted up string, trying to unravel the weeded mess in order to find the end. My secret memories and feelings were so many and very deep that it felt impossible to find any source of this leech that was clinging to my soul.

Although I was not abused, and had not done anything I was really regretful of, the contributing factors were subtle, insidious things that were difficult to pinpoint. Surely the bulimia itself didn't hesitate to contribute to the impact of it, but it went even deeper than just the effects of years of an addiction. Most of us would rather cowardly isolate ourselves than to let go of the grip upon our secrets. Even though my self-confidence ebbed away year after year, I longingly hoped that those memories would become but an illusion and soon dissipate into thin air.

Ever since I could remember, I felt out of place in a group, unusual—like I didn't fit in. *I'm just different,* I used to say to myself to excuse my unsettled feelings and insecurities, yet I was hiding something—an inner anxiety that I wasn't good enough and was not fully lovable. Of course my bulimia reinforced that lie by marking me as a dirty, disgusting girl who appallingly vomits in every way, shape and form. I knew I had felt this even before I was fifteen when the bulimia started.

My insecurity and anxiety influenced how I related to the world and I couldn't fully relax in the presence of others. I was always a little on guard, even with my closest friends. Small periods of time escaped when I was truly myself and free to be me, but the iron gate was easily dropped if I felt myself in danger of getting too close to someone. Now of course, those who didn't really know me could not tell the difference. "She is such a nice girl, and so friendly and kind" they would say about me. Did they really know me? Did I even know me? How could they know me if I didn't even know myself?

Lasting intimate friendships were a challenge for me, despite my deep longing to connect with them despite the fact I had many friends. During conversations that were leading toward talking about how I felt about my family, myself or other sensitive topics, I would shut down and dissociate from my feelings. My subconscious, and sometimes even conscious fear of being discovered and known, and thus potentially being ultimately rejected and alone caused this shutting down.

Why did I have so much shame? Besides having to hide the food habit on a daily basis and sneaking around to ensure it stayed hidden, I had other hidden secrets. No one knew how out of control I felt, or how insecure I really was at times; nor had they any clue that I was afraid to face my inner pain I felt within my family. I never admitted to the fact that I was afraid to date a guy for too long lest it gets real serious, nor how uncomfortable I felt about expressing my femininity and showing my developing body. I was also afraid to fail and fall below the standard I had set for myself at things that were important for me. Furthermore, I was certainly afraid that someone would discover that I didn't have it all together.

Shame often seems to bind us so that we feel unable to reach out for help. I felt alone, disconnected, and at times paralyzed in total fear. Ironically this lion's pit was preferred to risk sharing myself with another person. I was more comfortable in this pit than in the unknown hole I could possibly be in if I let my weakness be truly known by another. Somehow I thought I would crumble if I let my weakness show!

As I continued to get to the root of my shame, I came to see shame like a tumor that isn't meant to be ruling a person's life, zapping strength from a person's vitality.

I was sharing with my friend about this. "Kimmy, every time during my recovery when I would see all that needed changed in me, a flash flood of condemnation and fear would cover me. Shame was then everywhere around me, filling every crevice of my being. So, I decided to start looking at my sins, my bulimia, and my shame in a different light. I saw that all the things that didn't image the way God made me, were like a *tumor* on my body. As with all tumors, it sucks life and energy from the rest of the healthy body by hoarding the blood supply and nutrition from the rest of the body.

"So Kimmy, to get well, God wants us to cooperate with Him in getting rid of that tumor and to let His chemotherapy flow throughout the body to get rid of the enemy. Once we see shame in its right perspective, we can then fight to get well, fighting the tumor without really fighting or hating ourselves along the way."

I began to see shame for what shame was—an enemy that was robbing me of my inheritance, of the wonderful person whom God had created me to be. I realized that I was not a "dunghill" in the core of my person covered in God's grace, as Martin Luther once proclaimed, but a beautiful woman redeemed and set free by Jesus Christ's sacrifice of love. The core of a person's being is beautiful. By his sacrifice and grace, I am also being sanctified and freed from the strongholds and "tumors" that are still hanging on to me. By His mercy, one day in Heaven, when I'm home, I will fully reflect the image of Him as He created me to be!

God's redeeming grace makes it possible for us to stand tall once again, to let ourselves be known and discovered— even amidst recovery. As we share our secrets buried within us, new life and joy springs up in place of it. The fact that God knows our thoughts and every detail of our past, present and future, can liberate us to shed our heavy cloak of shame—forever.

Renouncing Inner Vows

So many of us have said, *I won't let anyone hurt me again*, or something like, *I won't ever get close to anyone again!* Inner vows that we consciously or unconsciously make throughout our life, even as a toddler can have negative effects on us as adults. It has been significant for me to renounce these inner vows that I had made throughout my life because they were unconsciously fueling my bulimic habits.

After I experienced an outburst of anger that caused me to physically hurt my little sister, I declared emphatically to myself, *I will never be out of control with my anger again!* I kept that vow. When I was older, I even convinced myself that I didn't have any anger within me because, as I used to tell people, "I'm not an angry person". I needed to let go of this vow once I began seeing my need to learn how to feel my anger.

Inner vows are made to protect ourselves in some way. For example, I made that vow to not be angry again because I saw how much I had hurt my sister and I knew it was possible to do it again to her or someone else. I was afraid of myself and I wanted to protect others from myself. Some of my inner vows were uncovered without me being aware of them. They were broken simply by maturing and making good decisions. There were others I needed to work prior to being set free.

Here are some of my other vows:

I will never get married if marriage is like that!
I will not be vulnerable like that to anyone again!
I will not trust any men.
I will never be a burden to anyone!

Do you ever wonder why you feel compelled to do a certain thing? It may be because of a vow you unconsciously made long ago.

There came a time when I needed to renounce these vows I once declared. I had to understand the original purpose of that vow. How did it protect me? Now that I am an adults and can protect myself in a healthier way, I can declare that I am willing to be hurt again, to be rejected again and misunderstood for the sake of a greater good. This releases the vow of self-protection.

Because I had closed myself off to marriage out of self-protection and wanted to be open, I had to risk getting hurt by a man. If I never took that risk, I may never enjoy the beauty and wonders of that friendship. When I renounced those vows I made toward men and marriage, I grew to fall in love with the vocation of marriage and presently have many great friendships with men.

Let me take you through a conversation I had with a good friend recently that will illustrate my point. She was struggling with losing weight, as I had several years back. She couldn't figure out why she hadn't lost any weight, although she was still bingeing occasionally and always felt bad about her body. I suggested that it could be because of some inner vows she had made at some point in her life to stay overweight as a protection against men.

She had been date raped and hurt in subsequent relationships by guys. It was understandable why she was protecting herself from being hurt again. If she wanted to be thin, she had to become aware of what was holding her back from letting go of the weight and then be stripped of any inner vows, thus replacing them with truth. It demanded a great vulnerability on her part to move on from this place. I shared with her what I worked through.

At one time during college, I was 25 pounds over what I felt was a comfortable weight and I couldn't seem to shed the extra pounds. I was bingeing occasionally, but exercising moderately. I struggled within myself to see what was holding me back, of my possible fears I had of being thin. I remembered an inner vow I had made some time during high school when I was thin and was becoming more attractive to men and experienced them whistling and jeering at my body. Feeling disgusted and not knowing how to combat it, I found that through purging I felt "protected" from feeling sexually vulnerable to men.

Purging made me feel disgusted with myself and less attractive to men. I had unconsciously vowed to not let myself be vulnerable to men. I felt shame for hiding the bulimia from others and for being prey to men. Yet in a sense, I made this vow for a "good" reason—to keep myself pure and virgin.

I was afraid of being attractive to men and all the consequences that might follow. I had many questions like: *Would I end up in a shameful relationship because of a man taking advantage of me? What would my family think? Is it normal and good to like their attention?* I was afraid to hear the answers to those ominous questions because I would be forced to deal with them. It was easier to hide behind the self-protective wall than to face it.

What I was truly afraid of was losing control and letting my emotions loose and possibly having to live with them controlling my life. This, I thought, could lead me into a wild life of sexual promiscuity. This fear reinforced the lie that there actually was something awful inside me, a part of me that could break down this image of the good girl I believed myself to be. These fears prevented me from letting go of the extra weight I had put on, and from stopping the purging for good. To give up both meant I would have to make myself vulnerable to men and learn how to care for myself in a righteous, godly way.

It was over ten years since I had made that vow when I realized that I needed to face the fear of being thin again, thin without the purging. Once I confronted this inner vow, I had to practice in my mind what it would be like to be thin. I pictured myself walking down the street, looking nice, and having some guy whistle and jeer at me. As I imagined this, the feelings of self-disgust welled up, and a self-hatred spilled out.

Then at that very point, I stopped myself. *Katie,* I thought, *they are not whistling at YOU, they don't know you. They are perverse men being obnoxious, fulfilling their own lust and desires. They don't know what it means to respect a woman. They are only hurting themselves and God. They cannot hurt you because you are protected. There is no shame you need to receive from them. Be at peace.* Little by little such work helped me feel comfortable around men.

Curses are another form of a vow that can keep us bound. Sometimes these can only be discerned through prayer, although sometimes things are fairly obvious. If there is a line of alcoholism/addiction, suicide, depression or abuse your family, it is possible that there may be a generational bondage in those particular areas that predisposes you to certain tendencies, thus making you more vulnerable to falling into certain areas of sin. If you have an opportunity for someone to pray with you for the healing of any possible bondage in yourself and family, it may prove well worth the time. God can break the pull toward that destructive area in your life.

One of the most common self-condemnations I've heard is, *I will never be good enough.* This can become a curse and can contribute to feeling restless and dissatisfied with the situation around us and with ourselves. Some people are told this lie over and over by significant people in their lives.

On the other hand, we can also make good vows and blessings upon ourselves, ones that edify us and build our character. For example, *I DO want to seek you, Lord, with all of my heart. I do want the direction of my heart to be toward You alone.* By making these affirmations, we are able to face ourselves head on and to take a deeper responsibility for our lives. This then allows us to begin more actively restoring our relationships with those around us.

Calling a Spade a Spade

Recovery involved working through damaged relation-ships. Most of the time I did not see the changes I longed for in those who hurt me. This did not stop me from growing, nor did it stop me from loving them. My responsibility was to repent from my part in the relationship. I needed to deal with this order to grow.

Forgiveness of other people's sins is crucial to living the Gospel. Once I admitted my anger, rage and disappointment toward the sin that others had committed toward me, I could truly forgive the hurt I experienced. Forgiving others, which is done only by God's grace, will set our hearts free. St. Ephraem who lived in the Third century said, "Beloved, do realize that if we are in enmity with someone, in vain do we raise up our hearts to God while we are at work."

All through the Gospel, Jesus emphasizes the importance of heart-felt *metanoiah*—which is the Greek word for repen-tance. Metanoiah means to change. We must change in such a way that we are turned around 180 degrees. This change in direction will only lead us to fulfill more solidly our hearts desire which is to live life more fully and with new vibrancy in Gospel love. Each time we set our hearts right, we are restoring our relationship to God, society and ourselves.

> Repentance is facing what is true: I am a sinner and double-minded. And I deserve to be separated from God. It is a deep recogni-tion that life comes only to the broken, desperate, dependent hearts that longs for God. It is a melting in the warm arms of God, acknowledging the wonder of being received when it would be so understandable to be spurned. It is taking our place at the great feast, eating to our fill, and delighting

in the undeserved party being held in honor
of our return. (The Wounded Heart p. 217)

Ouch! Those are harsh words! I thought. It was important for me to be open to repenting not only for the bulimic
actions, but for all of the other things including self protection, self destruction, a wrong concept of God, a wrong
pride, self independence, a will that refused other people's
help and loving support, and many other sins. Heaping more
coals of fire upon myself was certainly not the goal. Rather,
I longed for freedom. The truth will set us free. This
increased freedom to receive the love of God in my life
allowed me to love others and myself more fully.

Real repentance restores relationship and reaffirms a
desire for intimacy. Elizabeth Elliot, a missionary and
speaker once said, "It is only as we take a hard, clear look at
sin that we can open our hearts to the need of the cross. The
necessity of the Cross of Jesus Christ." She went on to say,
"Calvary is the estimate of God's hatred of sin. In order for
me to know who I am, I must know God, and I must accept
His judgment." His judgment is surely an expression of His
severe mercy.

I found many reasons not to enter into repentance. One
reason was that I feared punishment. I saw God as constantly pointing the finger, ready to lay another set of rules
and regulations on my already overburdened shoulders. *I'll
do my own thing if You are that way!* I would shout inside
myself. Others times I seared my conscience to such an
extent that the sin was not even sin anymore. Hidden
beneath the rubble though was a callousness and resistance
to change. Other fears of repentance included a fear of
letting go of control, stubbornness and a strong will.
Sometimes I lacked faith that a certain habit or sin could
actually go away. *Why repent and try to change? The
change won't last anyway.* I thought.

My road toward repentance and reconciliation was not easy. I needed to admit I had wronged another person and take responsibility for the neglect of my actions. When I recognized sin as sin, I was faced with a choice: Will I consent to changing? Do I want to change? What direction will that take me if I decide to change? Am I ready to give up my life in whatever way I need to in order to set my life on this new path? For so long it was easier to not face any of these questions and abstain from defining any sins in my life.

We are fooling ourselves when we think that God is not "angry" that we sin by bingeing and purging and hiding all our pain. This anger is not the same anger most of us are accustomed to. God's anger flows from His relentless love for his beloved child. Actually it's not really even anger; it's the fire of His passionate love. Just as a mother is upset and talks sternly to her son for running into the street over and over to fetch his ball, so, too, are God's discipline and anger signs of His care for us. He tells us, "...Or do you hold his priceless kindness, forbearance and patience in low esteem, unaware that the kindness of God would lead you to repentance?" (Romans 2:4)

I needed to see God as He really is and also to "hate what is evil" as it says in Romans 12:9. For me to really hate my bulimia and the disobedience I was living out, I needed to have a like mind to God and hate the sin but love the sinner. I didn't want to fall into hating it in a human sense, otherwise there was the danger that I would destroy myself in the process and never separate the sin from the sinner. Most bulimics I have talked to despise the evil of their addiction but also hate most every aspect of themselves with a passion that only brings death to their souls.

God's perspective is so much greater and is nothing like ours. His passion to love will repel anything that is evil will bring life and freedom to our souls. God is good and cannot even hate, but His incredible compelling love seems like hate against our sin; but it's not. It's the power of limitless love.

He cannot tolerate whatever destroys goodness in His beloved children and what obscures the image of God within us. He is satisfied with nothing less than for us to be free of those things that keep us from union with Himself.

Nothing can change the fact that we are made beautifully, uniquely and wonderfully, but a lot can obscure and hide who we are and it breaks His heart to see us destroy ourselves! It makes Him angry at the sin to such a degree that He sent His only Son to suffer and die an agonizing death in order to give us the option to be set free from this spiraling rampage of self-destruction. For He loves us and sees all that we are and can be.

I am sometimes afraid of God's love because it means if I accept it, I must face a decision to change. And sometimes I don't to change. If I accept He loves me I know I will be drawn to want to be in union with Him. If that is true, nothing unholy can be united with Him who is holy. Thus, I must let myself be purified by sweet fire.

Facing God's passionate love and gaining His perspective on sin, thus taking responsibility for our sin will bring us freedom. We have the choice to dare to accept it.

We are often like an old dusty cabin window that has mud, and maybe even a bit of bird dropping on it. If you turn your head in just the right direction, you can see a portion of the trees, sunshine and flowers outside in the meadow. For the most part, though, you can only see the blur of what is showing through the glass, and the light barely comes inside the room to warm you.

If you're like me, you love a good view and the beautiful outdoors! You rush to get the bucket of water and clean this filthy window. This takes time. The old cabin window hasn't been cleaned for several years, but in anticipation of the great view, you should excitedly labor away. At the beginning, it only looks worse, the obscurity gets more pronounced and you may wonder what mess you've gotten yourself in. You continue until finally the upper half is starting to look good and the warm light begins pouring in.

You may be tempted to give up because your arm is heavy from washing... but no! You'll know of the beauty outside, and you'll want to see it! So, plug away, washing, rinsing, washing and rinsing. You will even need to change the brown water because to make it perfectly clean, it need really clean water with a few drops of ammonia in it to prevent streaking. The last wash is just a refinement. After that is worked on for a while, you finally have the goal finished. Check out that beautiful sight! The room is filled with light and the sunshine warms your whole body. Ahhhh...This is how the window and view is meant to look!

Likewise, we can see our own sins as that dirt and mess on the window that is obscuring our view and keeps us cold from the lack of warm sunlight. We can become our own advocates like a watchdog for ourselves not letting anything harm our clear view.

There is life and joy that comes from true sorrow for our sins. There is no life in a false condemnation pouring out from a bundle of shame. If we hold tightly to our self-hatred and self-flagellation, we can never be free to enter into reconciliation, and we remain isolated, like someone sealed in a see-through box. For so long, I wore shame like a heavy wool overcoat laden with a large "GUILTY!" sign. Until that shame is healed, and we are clothed with a right-weighted sorrow for our sins for which Jesus has paid the penalty of death, only then can we have courage to step into the room of restoration through reconciliation. Tears can then flow that bring healing and life, not death.

As the years progressed, I began reconciling to my family and those closest to me. Although it was very painful at times, what a gift it has been! I began to recognize their own humanness, taking them down from the pedestal that I had put them on which demanded that they be perfect. I began to see that *I* was the one that needed to change, since they may never change to meet my particular needs. I can change how I respond to things that habitually irritate or hurt me.

My family didn't need to change in order for me to be free. *I* had to change the way I related to my family and had to get more real. Now, I am more accepting of who they are and what we are able to share with one another. I can now say that I feel "at home" with my blood family, despite all our many differences and I look forward to growing in love for each of them in the future. Taking responsibility for my sins and defects has enabled me to move on and build relationships with my family that has been so wonderful!

Examining my heart has now become a daily routine. Certainly I do not do it in a scrupulous manner anymore that causes anxiety and inflexibility but in a way that leads me to keep my heart free and pure. By examining my heart, I keep on top of anything that may drag me down. Sometimes there are unconfessed sins, other times, I've been hurt by someone and not acknowledged it and let it fester, other times there is a spiritual cause and I just need to take time to praise God in song. As we get to know ourselves better, we will learn what tends to bring us down, the areas or outside influences that set off our weaknesses and lead us to feel unrest and depressed. Then we can more easily get through those hard times and not let them weigh us down more than is necessary. Through this type of recognition, repentance and reconciliation, we will continue to grow and keep the view out of our window clear and beautiful!

Choose Life!

I have experienced numerous episodes of inner healing. What I mean by that term is the times of emotional and spiritual restoration from things within me that were out of order or hurt. They are unexplainable touches by God in my heart and mind, like an inner surgery that occurs silently yet completely by the Holy Spirit. They are little gifts from God that strengthen and repair our soul from acquired damage. Inner healing came through many different avenues.

Sometimes, it would happen when I was walking alone in the woods, or while waiting for a bus in the inner city. Other times it came through the love of a friend, or during fun times with other people. There were many little and some big things along the way that made the difference at certain points in time. Mostly it came quietly and gently through times in my own prayer and in friendships with other people.

One such time was when my Franciscan University dorm director, Sr. Jean prayed with me. For several months prior to that, I felt a gnawing urge to be open to healing for the time when I was within my mother's womb. Every time I heard the word, "fetus", I felt uncomfortably anxious and didn't know exactly why. I began noticing over the next few weeks that for so many years I had felt an unexplainable anxiety that seemed always a part of me. At certain times I would have slight panic attack which caused me to freeze up inside for no particular reason. I often felt that same anxiety and panicky feeling when I spoke of being in my mom's womb.

At first I thought this connection of the anxiety and my time as a fetus was very strange and that I was just making it up. Sometimes when a parent doesn't want a child, the fetus senses this rejection, but my Mom and Dad were certainly very eager for me to be born, (they wanted six kids!) and so she never thought about abortion. In fact, I admire and am grateful for my parent's determination to keep trying to have children despite my mother's miscarriage after I was born and after serious uterine problems in the following years. My parents surely taught me to respect life, particularly Mom who worked for Right to Life counseling for many years. So I knew the source of this tension was hidden and deep, if it even existed at all.

I brought it all before the Lord in prayer. He knew what I needed. When Sr. Jean and I prayed together regarding this, I began experiencing something being released in me and I wept within the deepest parts of my soul. God was touching me. As we prayed for God to heal anything within me that went on while in my mother's womb, I had a picture of myself: I saw myself not wanting to come out when it was time to be born. I wanted to stay in the womb. In the womb I seemed to know God who created me. I knew His peace and love, and I didn't want to leave that nice place to come out into the anxious world. I was thus mad at God for letting me out. I was afraid at what I might experience.

Even before this time of prayer, I had at times felt a strange urge in me that I didn't want to live. It wasn't as if I hated life so much that I wanted to kill myself, but some strange drive pulled me into the direction of longing to cease to exist on earth and to be at peace.

Maybe I had sensed, even in the womb, the state of anxiety existing in the outside environment and I wanted to get away from it, but healing doesn't depend on knowing the details of what caused the anxiety. Now some may think this is fruity, but there was a deep knowing that this experience was true. Yet, it is also possible that God was using this image to heal me and bring before Him my anxiety and pain I had accumulated through the years of bulimia.

Nevertheless, we both recognized that my desire not live was buried within me. I had always felt squirmy and restless when I read the verse in Deuteronomy 30:19, "I have set before you life and death, the blessing and the curse. Choose life, then, that you and your descendants may live." Even though I was a Christian who should be embracing life, there was something in me that wanted to die. I didn't know why I felt this. I was embarrassed and shameful feeling this way. Maybe it had something to do with not wanting to face the world outside the womb and being caught in the death of bulimia or maybe I had just developed this sense somehow as a child. I don't know exactly *why* I was feeling this deep within, but it was important for me to renounce that desire to die.

In faith, I then repented for not wanting to live, and for the ungratefulness I had for the life God gave me. I then made a decision to embrace life and to be grateful for what I had been given. Since this prayer time, I have never experienced that same panicky feeling again; I've truly been healed of it.

I thank God for relieving me of that because I didn't know how horrible it was until it was gone and I lived without it for a while. God wants us to find our home within ourselves so we can feel more comfortable living in the world. God heals us in layers, deeper and deeper, little bits at a time. It takes patience and sensitivity toward ourselves to let this healing come about. The damage didn't come overnight; so don't expect the healing to either.

Many times I blocked opportunities for healing. Now I can see that I could not blame God for that. Sometimes it's just because I was not ready to receive the healing. I thought I knew God and myself in a complete way, but instead I was deceiving myself. I held onto my obscured perceptions and ideas about others and myself because of my insecurity to let go of them. I chose instead to stay in the comfort of my sickness for fear of accepting something different and new. At times I feared I would lose control if I changed too much or too fast.

There were many things that acted as blocks to receiving healing. They included a failure to receive or extend forgiveness toward others, to myself or to and from God, a failure to accept my weaknesses, and fear of what I may find out about myself. Overshadowing all of these was my erroneous perception of God's character. Harboring a wrong concept of God can keep us from giving our hearts fully to Him. For example, I was rebellious towards God for a while because I thought that if this is the God whom I am supposed to follow, forget it! Once I asked God to heal that wrong conception of God. I began experiencing God for who He really was. I wanted to then follow him from the depths of my heart. Until such issues are confronted, sometimes healing can't progress. A healed self will is anxious to collaborate with God.

I was at times afraid of receiving goodness and blessing from the Lord and other people because I thought that if I enjoyed the good things, I would long for more goodness and blessing from them. This then would deepen our friendship, which would in turn cause me to be more vulnerable and therefore open myself to be hurt. It was easier to protect myself from receiving too many blessings. Goodness melts the walls of stone in our hearts and therefore can be threatening to fragile hearts. God waits patiently for us to open our doors each step of the way, for He will never force Himself upon us.

I had to train myself to receive God's love and care. At one of the support group meetings I attended, sponsored by Jackie Barile, I was taught how to care for the "child within" and to "parent myself" as they called it. Jackie herself is a recovered bulimic. Not only did I need to learn to let others care for me but also firstly I had to care for myself and nurture that weak part of myself.

Learning to let myself be cared for by people took a lot of time and effort. I am still learning lessons in that area. I used to always squirm when I heard the word, "needy". Yuck! I was bound and determined to not be needy for anyone. I had made a decision in high school to not be a burden on my family which I maintained until I revealed my bulimia secret that one Christmas, five years into my eating disorder. I felt I fulfilled that vow very well.

Yet, I failed to recognize the fact that we all need one another, and we are designed to live interdependently. Our most basic need and longing is to be loved and respected and we need one another to fulfill that need. We are all created with needs, whether we acknowledge them or not. Some people are more needy than others, but we all have them and they are not shameful.

I used to feel so panicky inside and felt alone and in need of deep care; but that is a normal response, particularly for someone who has cut herself off from other people. We are not meant to live in an isolated vacuum. We need to stay connected with people, even if it's only one or two persons. No matter how far or hard we run (inside or outside) we will never be alone because people *do* care. We may not choose to recognize it or accept what is being offered to us, but it is true. Nonetheless, out of fear, many of us try to run.

For so long I had felt loved by food and bulimia. It needed me and I needed it. It was my closest friend. If I felt excited, instead of calling a friend, I'd turn to food. If I felt lonely, instead of putting time into developing friendships, I'd call on my food friend. If I was angry and was afraid to confront someone, I'd go binge. If I was simply bored and didn't know what to do, guess which friend I'd call... bulimia.

Food didn't yell, criticize or reject me. I didn't have to worry about being vulnerable to it. It was soothing going down and coming up. It gave me a high that I was addicted to and I could control it—or so I thought.

Yet as time went on, it didn't serve me as it had in the beginning. Instead, it began causing me more pain than it was worth. I knew I needed to replace it with better things— I needed a new friend. I began learning to become open to accepting love from my family and friends. I had grown so self sufficient through the years and had closed myself off while struggling with bulimia, that I felt anxious around other people. I knew that the walls I had built up between my family and friends needed to be taken down. I needed sisterhood. I needed my parents. I needed friends.

I had never realized the blessing of "family" before recovery. At various times, I've feared being a "burden" on my family and other people. Yet, there is an often appropriate burden that we as humans must accept that we are to one another, a burden that acts as a gift to others, even when it causes us to sacrifice for the good of the other. The times I have confided in friends or family and shared my needs, it made me feel much closer to them.

After I left the hospital in '87, my older sister, Sue offered me help. "Kate, if you need *anything*, just let me know. If you want to go to a certain University to finish school, I will get a loan out and help you through school. Just ask; I want to help you!" That touched me so much! She was so sincere, and a real sister to me at that time when I really needed her support. That brought so much healing to me.

Since that time, I have come to better treasure my friendships and family. We need people, there's no way around that fact. We are made to live in community and to belong somewhere. One way to help yourself express your feelings and learn to be interdependent is through self-help groups. There are Bulimics Anonymous meetings, eating disorder support groups, Adult Children of Alcoholics, Alateen meetings and many others. Find one you click with and build a support network. There maybe is a share group at your church or school you can plug into. Learn to call a friend so that you can learn other ways to deal with what's going on. This will allow you to make better choices.

Being able to hear stories of other bulimics and compulsive eaters at Overeaters Anonymous meetings has helped me accept help from others and to grow in vulnerability. I learned especially through them that it's OK to accept my weaknesses and admit them. I saw them loving me amidst my pain and in my times of addiction. They were willing to serve me, which helped me to get outside myself to serve others and to love myself better.

Seeing the effects of the bulimia in relationship to those who care for us can often inspire us to be open for help to change. There are consequences to every choice. Every purge cycle will have a consequence whether you acknowledge it or not. Those effects will build up over time and end up hurting you and those you love.

Along with support groups, a counselor who you can relate to and has experience with bulimia is helpful during certain seasons of your recovery. They can help you get through some barriers to recovery a lot quicker than you can on your own. Find someone you feel comfortable with. If the counselor you have now doesn't work well for you, ask other bulimics for references to another counselor.

My good friend, Cathy who is a wonderful counselor said, "Remember, there is a season for counseling and a season for not receiving counseling. The role of a therapist is to provide support so that you can begin the hard work of looking at those feelings, emotions, fears and memories that you have been working so hard to avoid through the eating disorder. Sometimes we need help to become aware of the blockages so that we can take responsibility for making a change. They cannot make the change happen, but they can stand by you and cheer you on as you begin to take the risk to change."

Counseling showed me that I needed to be more open to take advice from people. I would always "listen" and be "open", but I had a narrow, tunneled vision of the way I thought I should go, and no one was going to stop me. I figured it was between God and me, and everyone else should keep their nose in their own business! When I examined my reaction more closely, I realized that I reacted so angrily because I assumed that people were giving advice because they thought I was stupid. In response, I would resist the advice so as to keep my image that, *I'm not dumb! I'll be in control because I know what's best for me!* Yet, as I grew more secure in myself, I was able to see and receive the wisdom that my parents and friends gave. I have my Dad to thank for giving me advice to choose Nursing rather than something else I was studying.

By receiving help in this area, I was able to relax a little more. Admitting my faults and mistakes was easier because I accepted that I didn't have to have my act all together in order to be OK. Saying, *I don't know* became easier and I did not feel bad about it. I also felt more comfortable with people disagreeing with me. This was a big growth for a people pleaser! Best of all, I don't have to binge and purge over people not agreeing with my decisions, or hide myself by acting wiser than I actually am!

Yet, above all relationships, the one I depend on the most is my relationship with God. Only as the cross is maintained practically and centrally in my life will I stay free. My interdependence with others is overshadowed with my relationship with my God. Without a relationship with Jesus, I would be tempted to depend on people to fulfill my need for peace, security and love.

I've learned to accept that people fall short and disappoint me, even when they have the best intentions. I certainly do it at times to others. Although it's never easy, I've learned to deal with them in a healthier way. But when I'm not putting my security in Jesus, I lean toward finding it in other things—friends, ministry or as it was for many years, food. The victory is that now I can recognize it and then go to God in prayer to ask for grace to get back on track with Him. I am not without hope anymore!

CHAPTER SEVEN

Hidden Secrets

S eeing the effects bulimia had on my relationships was
very much intertwined in facing my need to become
more vulnerable.

*Would God want me to be so needy? Was it OK to feel so
lonely and admit that I long for deep, meaningful relationships? Was it shameful to long to be loved tenderly and
respectfully by a man, and in turn want to give myself fully
to someone? Was it selfish to expand my nursing talents in a
way that would bring satisfaction to my work?* So many of
these concerns consumed my thoughts.

Resentment, bitterness and even rage against God for
not providing us with the longings of our hearts, or anger at
certain people for failing our expectations is a temptation.
The anger will eat us alive. Unfulfilled longings are part of
life. I had to learn to trust that God is good and He loves me
even if I do not understand the circumstances.

I think one of the hardest areas has been to admit my
need to receive love from people. The word "needy" just
used to tick me off. To admit in high school that I needed a
counselor's help was somehow embarrassing. Why?

Because I had built up an image of myself that was almost Superhuman. And superhuman people don't "need" anyone.

Yet I later I realized it was all a facade. Many people do go through life managing somewhat effectively by never really depending on anyone. I discovered the loneliness of this lifestyle. It was as if I was only half alive.

God gave me all these longings and desires to be loved, to love and to know myself. Once I acknowledged and accepted them, I felt free to be me. I still had a lot work to do at learning to love myself if I was to fully express my longings.

I was plagued with a siege of self-destructive thoughts that churned night and day. Giving into a rage of purging only silenced the clamor for a few hours, and sometimes only for a few minutes. I generally liked myself, and thought I was a pretty good person, yet the longer I was bulimic, the worse was my self-image. Bulimia is like a slow leaking bottle of poison within a person, toxically destroying the very life of that victim. As the years progressed, I helplessly watched my self-esteem deteriorate after every binge and purge.

I only loved the part that looked good, but I hated the rest. I admitted that I was too hard on myself, and began seeing how it didn't pay off to be that way. I used to think it was "good therapy" to beat myself up mentally during volleyball training. I was convinced that this was the best way for me to improve myself.

Yet after I failed at almost everything I was doing— volleyball, schoolwork and relationships, it was obvious that I needed a new approach. I knew that God loved me, my parents and sisters loved me but did I really love me? The answer was obvious.

When I started to believe that the negative talk was constructed from lies, the negative talk started to lose its power. I needed to make a firm commitment to stop beating myself up for mistakes, stop yelling at myself and begin to speak compassionately toward myself. Even after binges and purges I had to stop killing myself with the silent beatings.

I began accepting compliments paid by others with a simple, "thank you", acknowledging my talents, even though inside I would cringe at the kind words. I made more efforts to be outgoing and began making friends, despite my tendency towards introversion. I still felt I was fat, and had gained some pounds after stopping the purging, but I began speaking lovingly about my body and touching it with kindness. I knew I had to become friends with my fat and give up the war with those fat cells on my hips, arms and stomach. I knew that even if I were at a good weight, it would never be good enough in my mind's sick eyes.

I was afraid to become thin without having the bulimia as a guard over my thinness. If I was honest, I didn't want to lose weight. Being thin and not bulimic would open a whole array of feelings and challenges that I was not ready to handle. Guys would make sexual comments. They would want to date me. I may give in physically in ways I wouldn't be happy with...I would look good.

I had to work at accepting the possibility of losing weight. I made efforts to accept all my fears, gently talking to myself saying, *I know you can't handle this now, but one day, you will feel OK to let go of the fat. Not now, but one day. Either way you are making a choice.* If I did purge, I would sit and talk to myself, checking out how I was feeling and comforting the child within as a loving mother would for her hurt child.

At first I thought by being so gentle on myself I would only be condoning what I was doing and the symptoms would not improve. Yet it had the opposite effect after some months. To my surprise, I began developing a real compassion for myself that I had never had before. I needed to be friends with myself, knowing that a good friend would feel sad that I was bingeing and purging. She would long with love for that person to be freed. I kept the dream alive that one day I would be free.

One of the other things I did was to write little notes and write things like, "Kato, I love you!" "You are beautiful inside and out, Katie" and "I like you, Katie" (Sometimes it's nicer to simply be liked rather than loved!) Then I taped those notes in strategic places like my car dashboard, the bathroom mirror, beside my bed, and inside my prayer book.

I remember the first time that I was really moved after reading the note on the bathroom mirror. My insides squirmed as I forced myself to say, *Kato, I love you!* Immediately after that last word was spoken, a litany of harsh rebukes followed, *You do not! You're a jerk! Look at how many times you have binged and purged today! You're a disappointment!* ...and on and on.

Certainly, those harsh thoughts sprung from my wounded mind and "the Accuser", the devil. Yet, it was my responsibility to see that those lies didn't control me anymore and that I put my thoughts under the proper authority-under Christ. Jesus died so that I could be free of such mental bondages and that I wouldn't have to be a slave to those lies or idols. The chains on me were broken once I was baptized and accepted Christ as my Savior, I just had to learn how to daily walk out of the shackles. No one could change my thinking without my effort and permission. I happily gave the Lord permission to help me change. I admitted the need and desire to have good thoughts, thoughts that were truth, not lies.

After a few weeks, I began more confidently and boldly declaring what was written on my little scraps of paper posted around the house. The first time that I actually remember meaning what I was saying was in the bathroom. *Katie, I love you!* It brought joy and tears to my eyes to finally say it. I jumped up and down in the bathroom saying,

Yes! I do! Kato, I even LIKE you! You have a lot of good qualities, and you are going to one-day get over this bulimia. Hang in there!

Being my own advocate was wonderful. For the first time in a long time I felt more in control of my life. It was quite ironic that this took place in a bathroom; the very place the act of my bulimia ever began.

Still, there were more hurdles to climb in this area of self-love, as I later found out. As I learned more about myself and accepted myself, my love for God and others grew. The more I seem to try to give and receive love from others and God, the more I come to know and love myself, including my weaknesses and character quirks. Having a good self-esteem in the world's eyes is a bit different than having a good self-esteem as a Christian. Sadly, for some people, if you look good—you are good.

God's plan is so much more wonderful! It doesn't matter how you look because you are created in His image. You can show any weakness because not only will you grow in humility, but God will use it to show his strength. Being the King's princesses and princes provide a royal status that gives us dignity, honor and hope.

As I worked through each of the areas of my life that needed to be dealt with, and received the Lord healing touch, my self-image began to improve. I began to see that I was more than my bulimia. I was not "Katie the bulimic". I was Katie who struggled to overcome bulimia and who one day would be free from it. Part of that healing was to deal with my relationship and perception of men and marriage. Although difficult, I needed to face what I had hidden in my heart.

The Big Dark Box

I was not bulimic simply because I loved to eat. I certainly found no real pleasure in purging. There was though a deep hunger that I was trying to fill-to purge something I did not want to keep inside. If you don't deal with the roots of your addiction, you will never be truly set free.

As I became aware of the roots of my addiction, it was impossible to avoid one of the strongest, deepest roots: Fear of vulnerability. Why did I have such difficulty allowing myself to be vulnerable to people, particularly to men?

The fear was like a big dark box that I was afraid to open. I could somehow see it and even feel the eerie, cold atmosphere within and around this guarded cage. Although hidden deep within, the fear seemed to control most of my actions and thoughts, thus keeping me bound to its death grip. Bulimia and other self-protective behaviors seemed to be the guards of the cage, preventing me from seeing the monster within that subtly controlled my every move. I knew there was no way out but through this mysterious box. I had to break it open and destroy it if I wanted to move on.

I had no idea that it would be such an incredible challenge. During the counseling sessions, whenever Tom asked me about my relationships with certain people I was very close with or what my feelings were towards the men in my life, I would shut down inside and dissociate from my feelings. I felt vulnerable, dirty, threatened, scared and panicky while my demeanor would struggle to maintain a calm composure.

This is a sort of dissociation process, as psychologists call it, which we all exercise in order to deal with emotional shock and trauma. When used appropriately, it is a God given coping mechanism. For example, if we receive a call that a loved one has died, we somehow handle it. We are able to make arrangements to get to the hospital as soon as possible and be with that person and make any necessary important decisions about the matter. We are thus able to function at productive levels in a tragic situation, thanks to our dissociation ability. Later we will find ourselves falling apart.

I exercised this gift of dissociation to a self-destructive

fault. I learned to "click out" and fiercely guard myself when I felt vulnerable-which was most every situation! It felt like an invisible force shield that would instantly surround me. I could move freely about in, but was able to really touch another as much as I wanted and they could barely touch me in a heart to heart relationship. Tom was one of the few people who saw this invisible shield and with whom I allowed this shield to be lowered a few inches.

I began to notice how uncomfortable I would feel when I got close to any man. There was not even one man I felt safe around. "Katie—what are your running from? Is there something within you that you are not facing?" I used to hate that challenge posed to me from my counselor. What did he see in me that I didn't?

Then I began to wonder—why was I so tense? Was I abused at one time? Fabricated pictures of men or boys abusing me at a young age, fearful episodes of burglars breaking in the house or a family member sexually abusing me swarmed my head with efforts to fit them into a "hidden, dark memory", a sort of sealed box I may have blocked out for years. Was this true? Could it be I had forgotten a terrible tragedy in my life thus causing me to run inside?

Nothing ever clicked and I knew within the depths of my being that such incidences had never occurred. Yet I was still aware that I was running from something. Even though I had stopped the purging and most of the bingeing for a few years, I knew that this something was eating at the core of my being, still putting coals on the fire.

Once I consented to looking deeper within myself and at how I related to other people, particularly to men, a whole gamete of buried feelings began surfacing. I realized that I became friends with people only to a certain point of closeness, then I would become afraid and shut off my emotions and not let them get any closer.

With my girlfriends, I only let one or two people "in". If

the friend showed any signs that she was insensitive toward me or might reject me in any way, she would quickly be put on the "black list" and I would not let her back "in" for a long time.

The few times I did allow myself to date, I would break off the relationship within the first month saying, "I didn't feel anything for him anyway." When I became more physically attracted to a man, it would scare me and I would once again cut off the relationship in fear. I had built a guard around myself that protected me from getting hurt in any way, yet if I wanted to really love more deeply, those barricades needed to be knocked down.

The previous year, I had prayed a novena asking God if it was in His plans for me to get married. I had a very interesting dream on the ninth day and awoke in the night a bit shocked. In the dream I saw Jesus' face and He said to me, "You're afraid of marriage because you're afraid a man can never love you like that." I still remember the words and picture quite clearly.

What did Jesus mean by "that"? I realized that I never thought a man could ever love me purely—respectfully— truly lovingly. I believed that a man could only love me for his own selfish passions, and not out of genuine care for me. I did not believe a man could know me to the depths of my being, and love me deeply, despite my faults and failings.

What was I afraid of? I honestly didn't know. Rationally, I was not afraid of anything. I wasn't aware of any fears I had with men, my father or people in general. Subconsciously there were blocks. For example, I remember, during my freshman year at Utah, wearing my somewhat tight jeans, a pretty top and a great hairstyle and began walking down campus to class. My inner thoughts were self-destructive and reflected a self-protection that bulimia gave me. I thought, *I know I look good...but no one is going to want me because if they knew what I did with my food, they would be so disgusted they wouldn't come near me!* I could then keep men at a distance by persuading myself that I was unlovable.

The same thing happened when I was 25 pounds overweight. I protected myself by thinking similar thoughts, *At least I don't have to worry about them being attracted to me—I'm too fat for them.* In reality, they wouldn't have been open to me because they could see on my face that I didn't want them to get near me! I was afraid to be in a relationship with a man and it had nothing to do with how I felt about my body size or appearance. I was afraid of myself. Understanding such subconscious motivations to stay bulimic was like putting little candles up in that secret black box.

My counselor, Tom asked me, "Katie, if God calls you to minister to a priest or any other man, can you do it with an open heart?" I had to honestly answer "No way." He then challenged me to look at my relationship with my father. "Are you loving your parents as God wants you to?" "Yea— I do love them." I sheepishly said. "O.K., but do you love them passionately, totally with all your heart. That's the way God asks you to love them." Well, he could see the answer on my face—a big "No!" Facing what was behind that "No!" motivated me to work through any obstacles in loving my dad, and thus the barriers I had put up with men.

Hesitantly I looked at what may have adversely affected me. I was always my dad's little buddy. I loved to be with him and he was faithful to spend time with me (and I believe he loved it too!). He really supported me in all I did at school and in sports, attending most of my games throughout grade school, high school and when feasible, college.

Despite the fact of being assured of his love for me, there were some ways that his own weaknesses negatively affected me. I knew he would never do anything to intentionally hurt any of us kids, but at times, my father didn't instill in me a good sexual identity or a proper respect for women. My dad was not the only offender, as others reinforced such an image. The sweep towards a sexual revolution in society, magazines and TV all contributed. Although this combination may seem mildly destructive compared to todays, or even normal, it wounded the very core of my being.

Part of a father's role is to nurture their daughters in their femininity and confidence in who they are, along with protecting them against harm. When a father fails to do this it can subtly inflict damage. A mother and father's obvious trust, love and respect for each other gives the children inner and outer security and confidence in their relationships with other men and women, along with perspective and hope for their own future marriage. Part of my healing was to work through these areas.

As part of my work to overcome my fear of men, I used to carry around a picture of Jesus holding a little 4-year-old girl in his arms, a very tender picture. I wanted to be that child in Jesus' arms. Whenever I looked at that picture of the man, Jesus, holding the child, I cringed. I felt angry when I looked at that picture, yet I continued to practice the truth that God loves for me and wants to hold me like a child. *God is safe*, I kept telling myself. Over and over again I imaged myself feeling comfortable in Jesus' arms. Slowly my heart began to soften.

Dealing with my feelings toward men forces me to review my attitude toward marriage. It was clear to me that I had no desire to be married. Due to the occasions of conflict between my parents, and problems that married couples endure, I decided as an adolescent, to guard myself around men so that I would never go through the same thing.

I had to confront my anger and disappointment with the institution of marriage and the man I may marry one day. I didn't realize I had grown to hate and distrust men and be disgusted with any form of sexual contact or union of friendship. The part that I hated facing the most was that I still wanted their physical and emotional love despite such animosity. Such ambivalence was so irritating.

Tom cautioned me against protecting myself either by promiscuous behavior or by acting cold, since both reactions are controlling. God was challenging me to really give myself to someone with my whole mind and heart, not necessarily in a sexual way, but to give of my person. He encouraged me to be feminine, to allow myself to look nice and be open sexually, in the proper, godly sense of the word. Opening myself up to such passions was terrifying.

I realized that the only way I knew how to feel good about myself was to look gross, wear baggy clothes, and not open myself up to be physical with a man. In other words, to be cold, yet still be friendly. I was not comfortable with being a woman. Instead, I wanted to hide my tenderness and femininity for fear of being looked upon as an object, degraded by men's lustful desires. I was ruled by fear not freedom.

Our nation has bought into a bag of lies that keeps women and men in such a sad bondage, living for themselves and their own bodily passions. People are expected to have a health club membership and workout every day to meet the exaggerated standard of thinness. Consequently we become suckered into believing that we have to look and act a certain way in order to be loved by others. On top of that is piled the pressure to be regularly sexually active in order to be "in". All of this totally shrivels a woman's dignity and identity weakens the integrity of men.

The combination of the weight consciousness, insecurity in relationships with men, family instability, difficulty in expressing feelings, shallow friendships, and an addictive personality all set up a prime environment for me to keep hooked into bingeing and purging.

How did I actually work through this vulnerability issue? Firstly, I had to feel what I was feeling. I had to feel the shame, dirtiness and disgust with men and myself and not run from these awful feelings. I felt them and saw the images and memories of people who had hurt me. I worked at reprogramming my mind to see the situation as it really was, not as I experienced it. I used my creativity to reshape my distorted self-image and received healing from the Holy Spirit for the damaged emotions.

Let me show you an example of how I worked through this: I pictured a man off the street whistling at me and making obscene comments, looking me up and down as I walked by. I felt naked before his lustful eyes, dirty and trashed as he wished he could get a piece of me. Normally, I would walk away, adding one more brick to the wall around my hardened heart. As I endured the horrible feelings, I told my mind: This guy cannot hurt you. He is only hurting himself by giving into his lust. I would feel sorry for his poor wife if he had one. He doesn't see YOU, he only sees you as an object which you are certainly not. You are beautiful, pure and protected by God and not receiving that trash he is dishing out. I would then picture a clear shield between us so that his fiery darts could not touch me.

In cases where people close to me affected me, I had to allow myself to grieve over their woundedness that made them do what they did. I let myself feel the disappointment that our relationship was not all it was meant to be. For example, one time, a neighbor friend made some pretty rude sexual comments to me. My dad didn't say anything to protect me.

During counseling when such memories came back, I faced the anger, resentment, dirtiness I felt from such a close family friend, and also the disappointment that my dad didn't stop him from making his comments. As I grieved, and accepted the fact that these men fell short of their duty, I felt released from the bondage of that situation and God's healing replaced that pain.

There were many other memories and issues I needed to

work through, but the deep, dark black box began to be penetrated and disarmed.

We all know the potential side effects of an eating disorder. Some people with bulimia have unfortunately damaged their teeth and esophagus from the constant acid and their intestinal track from laxatives. Some people's hearts have been affected from the electrolyte imbalance, which has landed them in the hospital. Most everyone's concentration and rational thought processes are often severely impaired. Then there are some, God rest their souls, who aren't alive to share their story.

Nor can we forget the pain endured by family members and friends who watch us go through this and live with the pain that they can't fix us and make things better. There's no escaping suffering when living with an eating disorder.

Even though I didn't incur any known physical effects from the bulimic actions, I fell into my own vices of self-destruction. After the purging stopped after about 10 years of doing it, a new wave of feelings were coming to the surface that I had never felt. Everything within me wanted to avoid the deep anger towards others, the gut wrenching sorrow, neediness, jealousy, the awakened sexual attraction to men, longing for solid friendship and the homesickness. I felt like I was going crazy in this uncharted land of feelings.

I was working through a lot of tough issues with my counselor and resultantly felt like my emotions were bouncing off the walls. I was too afraid to express my neediness for a hug, to talk, or to cry with someone. At times I felt like screaming inside, and running away from the "me" I now was getting to know; but there was no where to run. Just eating food and not purging didn't give me the same high. Instead I turned my volcanic passions inward and began hating the source of all that I was feeling...ME.

Thus, the need to punish myself welled up within me, even though I was ashamed to feel that way. I was upset for number of reasons; my volleyball playing went sour, I had trouble confiding in friends, my relationship with my parents was strained and I felt so out of control. I was angry with men, too and felt uncomfortable about my femininity. I felt like a little kid inside at times wanting the love and support of older people and angry that I didn't have it. Deep down I just wanted to be held, like a mother holds their child and I was ashamed and hated myself for having such desires. My anger also masked the deep fear of who I was becoming.

I wanted to escape all this pain. Thus I found a new vice, a new addiction to avoid the inner pain. The physical scars on my arms, legs and abdomen will forever silently tell the painful story. This new vice, like the bulimia, worked for a short time to "relieve" myself from the inner pain. In the long run, though, it only caused many more problems. Any suicidal thoughts were motivations to experience peace within because I couldn't live inside myself any longer.

This new vice was the vice of physical self-abuse. For example, instead of feeling the pain of possible rejection from a peer, I would inflict physical harm to myself to keep from facing that pain of longing for friendship and disappointment of the rejection. It seemed easier to hurt myself physically, then to face the reality that in friendships we do hurt others and they will hurt us. I didn't have to focus on the emotional suffering, but on the physical pain.

It is similar to what bulimia expresses: "Overload!!!" Somehow, in a sick way, it felt good to hurt myself, because I was reinforcing the lies that I believed about myself. *Katie, you are bad within the core of you! Those you love are disappointed in you and are tired of you! You're different from everyone!* This was only another vice, like bulimia, that kept my guard up, so as to shut myself off from those I wanted to love and who wanted to love me.

I began to see that there was no limit or end to my

addictive self-destruction when I imagined even myself cutting off a limb, and *still* not being satisfied with the severity of self-harm. At this point I knew I was really sick in my mind, and I began taking the steps to face some of the pain from which I was running. If I didn't face myself and walk through the feelings, I would eventually destroy my very life. Going through recovery is a horrible feeling. At its low points, death can even feels like a better option. Although I wasn't suicidal per say, some times I just wanted to die.

Just as a child learns best if the parent provides a loving environment and positive feedback, so recovery will speed up as we learn to treat ourselves with dignity and respect-as God intends.

Reshaping My Body Image

My Grandma Julie, God rest her soul, was a beautiful looking woman both inside and outside. Although the photos are in black and white, any naked eye can see that she was a knock-out! She had a nice figure, deep ocean blue eyes with nice curly blonde hair. Yet there are some things I can't imagine her doing, which many young women think are normal, practices these days. For example, I can't see her standing in front of a full-length mirror pinching the extra skin on her hips and stomach exclaiming in disgust, "Julie! You are SO FAT! You're disgusting—!" Nor can I imagine her eating a hamburger and freaking out that it will soon be sitting on her thighs.

No way! Unlike so many people today, she would never have been so consumed with worrying about her body because she knew that was not the ultimate expression of herself. Although she became deaf at the age of seventeen, she was a confident woman whose identity was in the beauty within her, not what people thought of her. What has happened to subsequent generations to change for the worse?

To me, the answer is obvious. Society has tricked us into believing the lie that our bodies are the ultimate expression of who we are. So if you're not thin, toned and beautiful, society will tell you, "Honey, I got bad news for you! You're out'a here! Seeee ya! There ain't no future in your ball park. Girl, you better just hide yourself behind a desk and don't ever lift that big butt of yours off that office chair lest people notice your big-butt!"

Now, you laugh—but isn't this how we think? Isn't that how many people think? OK, maybe I over dramatized it a bit, but the point is well expressed, wouldn't you say? It seems that with men and women across the world, a sort of inner subliminal advertising is being uttered silently, yet deadly: *I hate my body. I am too fat here and too flabby there. I am not good enough to be loved until I am perfectly shaped. I want to be thin...I want to be thin...I want to be thin-thin-thin...*This outward goal of bodily perfection serves as a mantra that seeks to satisfy our deep, God given inner longings for love and life. I can only imagine that those who believe this fat sack of lies, will still be trying to lose weight on their deathbed!

Hatred of our body is only a symptom of the mess we've got inside. If we control our outside appearance, we may not notice how out of control we feel on the inside. Yet the self-hatred and unworthiness unleashes a pit-bull on the brain and emotions. We've got to make peace with our bodies, or we will never feel at home within or around ourselves.

Coming home to my body has been a significant challenge and victory. I was one who hated my body for so many years in high school and college. Although I was thin, I would grab any area that was not firm and rebuke myself for not ridding myself of this horrible default that seemed attached to my soul. It was insane. Reconciling my own body image and coming to a deep acceptance of it with all its faults, was key. There are some things that I practiced to facilitate this healing of my body image.

When I was in a department store, I would encourage myself to try on nice clothes and even bathing suits. Inside the dressing room looking at myself in the mirror I would tell myself positive things like, *It's OK to have a little fat there, or there. I don't have to be body beautiful. I'm OK as I am.*

While at home and changing my clothes, I would do the same. Seeing areas of my body I thought was fat, I knew I had to also love those parts of me. So, I would practice looking in the mirror at my "love handles", touch them and say, *Hips, I love you and accept you just as you are. I will no longer hate you or speak badly about you. I am sorry for hurting you for so long. In the right timing I will balance out to a healthy weight.* Then I would go to other parts of my body, which I despised and do the same. We must be reconciled with our bodies for healing, even when our bodies are grossly overweight. We must take responsibility and embrace our bodies genuinely and not psychologically disconnect our bodies from our self.

I decided to get on the scale less often and focus instead on how I feel. I challenge you to not weigh yourself as often (or at all!). Your body image is probably distorted anyway; so don't give control and power to a stupid scale. As you eat a normal, healthy amount, your body weight will eventually balance out to a God-given range. Mine is a few pounds higher than what my bulimic mind decided was good; but I feel best at this weight.

I need to mention here that some people's metabolisms are slow for various medical reasons. Some people have an imbalance in their thyroid hormone levels, causing them to not be able to lose much weight. Others have damaged their metabolism through anorexia for an extended period of time. Their bodies hold onto food in fear that they will again be starved, thus storing the energy consumed as fat. Be sure to consult a doctor and nutritionist if you are having any difficulties in these areas.

As we find out what normal eating habits work for us, the clothing sizes will drop as they need to drop. Or in some cases, will increase a little if they need to increase. Some of us have been underweight. Let go of the number of clothe size you wear. The ideal weight and clothe size I thought I needed was not accurate.

Our bodies are wonderful creations. In regard to eating habits, our bodies are our best teachers. They can tell us what food we need and don't need. This concept transformed my eating habits. I would practice asking myself, *Katie, what are you really craving?*

As I became aware of the answer to such questions, my taste buds awakened to the vast variety of fruits and vegetables that had so many vitamins and minerals. I found myself saying, *I'm craving fish, and wanting it because of the vitamin content my body knew was in it.* When I wanted a juicy orange, it was probably because of the vitamin C content. It was wonderful to become aware of my feelings of fullness that had for so long been repressed and to again reconnect with my body. I was able to eat some chicken, vegetables, and rice and be able so sit back in my chair and say to myself, *No thanks, I don't need any seconds.* My body was satisfied.

The sensation of hunger was amazing to experience. That was one feeling I had not felt for years. I was scared of it at first, and it was uncomfortable to feel. Yet I kept telling myself, *Katie, this is normal. Normal people feel this everyday. It won't kill you. Relax and feel it. It's good to feel it. Dinner will be in only one hour. This feeling will go away, and come back.* Our bodies are beautiful creations! I hope all people with bulimia can rediscover that their bodies are their friends and thus treat them as such!

I think one of the reasons we've become so body-centered is that our society has lost touch with what is really important in life. We are often too busy to sit and listen to people or to feel their pain. We are certainly too consumed with buying things for our so called "needs" that we've become ruled by the dollar bill and the endless maze of working to get more and working more to pay off what we got more of. We've become puppets to the media's sick standards of so called "beauty" that we've dulled our senses to *real* beauty—selling our pearl of great price for love of an outer image. Our society has once again demonstrated that the age-long pillars of evil of power, sex and money can motivate it. True beauty is on a different plane.

While in Sudan, I met a beautiful young Christian Sudanese girl in our village named, Angelina. She and her parents walked three days to our clinic to see if we could help heal her blindness. Her story was tragic. Seven months earlier, she was fetching water at the river and stepped on a land mine. Pieces of metal and acid flew everywhere, penetrating her two eyes and totally scarring her breast and abdomen along with spattering her thighs leaving her blind and terribly marred. Two days before this tragedy, she had pre-marital relations with a man whom she has never seen again and which left her pregnant. All she wanted to do was to die, particularly after we told her that medicine could do nothing to fix her blindness.

We prayed with her for Jesus to touch her eyes and spirit in hopes for a miracle. After the prayer, her tear-streamed face spoke to us of faith and courage. Although her eyes were still blind after praying, she chose to persevere amidst this horrific situation. She had no idea of how she would carry on her life in this state, but she knew she had to try.

Angelina is a truly beautiful woman. She really lives out her name. Beauty is something much deeper than what is seen on the outside—no matter how scarred we may be.

Let us take the challenge of life to discover true beauty, true wisdom. When is the last time you have really smelled a rose—so much that your nose tickles because the aroma overwhelms you? Have you recently looked out after a fall rain for the evidence of a rainbow across the sky? Have you felt the cotton tail of a bunny and even let it snuggle in your arms until its little racing heart calms down because it has finally rested? I've got too much to do in my life than to waste energy on pursuing a false beauty. Life is precious!

Please allow me to pray with you:

> Dear Lord, please always protect us from ourselves and others. God, give us strength to reach out and ask for that support from others and from You that we so desperately desire. Take away our shame and let us see ourselves with love and compassion as You do. Let these scars of ours be washed away by Your healing love. We are so needy of Your love, oh Lord... Embrace us now and forever, Father. Amen.

CHAPTER EIGHT

Fighting the Battle of Wills

I am surprised at how long it took me to admit that on my own strength I was powerless to win the battle going on inside me. I often told myself that I could quit this anytime; I just haven't tried hard enough. Deep down I knew I was quickly losing the war. It took time to let my will and affections be brought under the authority of Christ.

I always thought food and fat were the enemies. Later I came to see these were not the real opposition. The enemies I had to learn to contend with included my damaged emotions, societal pressures, Satan, and the greatest of enemies—my own stinking thinking. My emotional life flowed from my thoughts.

Although my own mind was my biggest foe, I knew that Satan played a part in my addiction. Jesus Himself called him a "murderer", a "liar and the father of lies" (John 8:44) Above all, the truth will always stand that, "Greater is He who is in us that he who is in the world." (1 John 4:4)

The devil didn't need to waste much time messing with me because the lies I had believed through the years about who I was, or wasn't, I was my own worst enemy. Anyone who might dare to live inside my mind even for five minutes would have been able to attest to the fact that my battle was won or lost in my head. No matter how rude and terrible the accusation was, I believed it.

Reprogramming my mind was essential. Though the following Scripture refers particularly to how we speak to others, we can apply it to how we speak to ourselves: "No foul language should come out of your mouths, but only such as is good for needed edification, that it may impart grace to those who hear. And do not grieve the Holy Spirit of God, with which you were sealed for the day of redemption. All bitterness, fury, anger, shouting, and reviling must be removed from you, along with all malice. And be kind to one another, compassionate, forgiving one another as God has forgiven you in Christ" (Ephesians 4:29).

Have you ever considered that you grieve your family and friends and God when you beat up yourself? It hurts them to see their precious one be unjustly yelled at and inflicted with verbal abuse.

The powerful drive to hurt myself by the bulimic habits, self destruction and negative self- talk were forces that often seemed overwhelming. I sometimes felt as if I was two persons-the Good Me and the Bad Me. I convinced myself that Bad Me wasn't really "Me". It was a fabricated being that was not meant to be a part of my life. The goal was to strengthen the Good Me, so that it could disintegrate the Bad Me. As the Good Me gained more control, then the degree of anxiety and confusion lessened and peace and security were replaced by it.

Slowly this coup took place. In the beginning though, there is so much internal fear in facing the Bad Me. It felt scary. It was as if the Bad Me monitored how much the Good Me could do and hates it when they begin gaining too much control. Victory came when the lies of the controlling Bad Me were disarmed. Reprogramming and strengthening the Good Me brought defeat.

Another strategy I utilized to defeat the self-condemnation was to agree with the accusations. This may sound funny, but it really began to work for me. To some degree, I could calmly agree with the harsh accusations that said, *You're so selfish!* With confident humility and absent of any shame or guilt, I responded, *Yes, there are areas I am sure that God will in his own time show me that I am selfish. I know I am not perfect, but I thank God He loves me and is making me perfect, each time I say 'Yes' to Him!* Then I could embrace myself knowing, "He who began a good work in you will continue to complete it until the day of Christ Jesus." (Philippians 1:6)

Other times I heard the negative part of my mind shout, *You're useless! You can't even hold a descent job or keep your life together! Look at how old you are and how old you are acting! You're worthless.* At times like that I said to myself, *True—I'm weak right now due to this sickness. I do have to depend on others to some degree to help me through this and people my age do already have kids. In the world's eyes, I am a bit worthless, but I don't care what society says. I know that in God's eyes and in the eyes of people who really know me, that I am O.K. I'm just weak, but I won't be like this forever. It's just a season. I will be a stronger person for having worked through all this. God loves me, and that other self certainly doesn't.*

What else can we do when we are hit with self-hatred and bad thoughts? Practice the presence of God, speak the truth, and learn Scripture responses. Don't give into negative self-talk. Fake it 'till you make it. Take responsibility for your part in fighting the battle, and leave the rest to God.

It's amazing to be able to bring every trouble, every worry and burden and every crazy thought to Jesus. We can lay it all at the foot of His cross knowing that His power and love can and will bring healing to us. There were many times I needed to bring the same burdens, the same insecurities to Jesus over and over and over again. Every time, He was there for me and little chips were knocked away in the boulder that kept the mental obsession blocked in me. He is also now right next to you, too.

Day In and Day Out

Many times, an everyday situation, or conflict seemed to unleash a truckload of uncontrollable emotions that came out of nowhere. When this happened, and I fell in a rut, I checked to se if it was a subconscious memory from the past that was being triggered. If it was, it was also an opportunity God allowed for me to be healed of something I had been carrying around for a while.

Maybe the fact that your boss reprimanded you has now caused a week of deep depression. Your boss possibly reminds you of a Second grade teacher who yelled at you in front of the class. Maybe it reminds you of your father or uncle. Check out what's at the roots. Don't quit your job out of a reaction, but deal with what that may be bringing up in you; otherwise you will find yourself in another similar situation in the future, and will you then run again, and again and again.

It's always good to know the enemy's tactics and weaknesses. In sports, this is the way to defeat the opposing team. You find where the opponent is weak in their defense and you take advantage of it over and over until you win. One of the biggest tricks our negative mind or the devil uses is to convince us we don't have anything valuable to give to others since we are consumed with bingeing and purging all day.

Even now, as a recovered bulimic, I'm occasionally tempted to believe that I am useless, particularly when I'm feeling down on myself. Yet, there is always something we can do for someone else. Even when we are down and out, maybe it's just one small thing we can give to another person who is worse off than we are. Even if we are so strung out from endless bouts of bulimia and obsessive thoughts, the most beneficial way to serve another person is to make our suffering into a prayer for them.

None of our suffering needs to go to waste. Some of the greatest saints were the ones who couldn't do much for others due to their incapacitation by a certain illness. Yet they prayed, "God, use my suffering as a prayer for those worse off than I." If we do such small act of kindness to someone, it will help us to keep our focus on the overshadowing main reason we are going through recovery. That is to be freed so to be able to be better lovers of God, others, and ourselves.

> "Now this is how we shall know that we belong to the truth and reassure our hearts before him in whatever our hearts condemn, for God is greater than our hearts and knows everything." (1 John 3:20)

Another one of my battle strategies was to learn to de-intensify myself. When I had made it through the bulk of recovery, I found that I didn't know how to be quiet, relaxed or peaceful inside. I was so used to operating with high levels of anxiety in my mind and body that it seemed impossible to slow down and not be so intense about everything.

I'm still learning how to do this but I've certainly come a very long way. Some people don't know what a good night's sleep is since for years even their sleep is a time of rigid anxiety. All I can say is that it takes time and practice to learn to relax, but it's important to develop this part of ourselves so that we can learn to enjoy life again.

It was comforting to know that I was not alone in this transition. Remember this: Jesus will never leave you, even when your head is buried deep in the toilet. One time I took

God at His word regarding this. I said, *God, You say you never leave us, but what about when I am purging? I can't believe you are standing with me near that toilet! You must at least turn your head away from me as I purge; it is so disgusting! Well, if you are there, then show me right now as I go to purge!*

I then pictured Jesus with me in that Utah dorm toilet stall that morning. I reached out my left hand to Him and I pictured Him even holding my hand as I leaned over that toilet vomiting. Yet it wasn't just imagery. I knew by faith that Jesus was there. To my surprise I did not see a face of disgust, but a face of pain that flowed out of His heart of love. Jesus was hurting for me, with me, his little sister. I saw His eyes well up with tears as He longed to see me free from this horrible bondage.

This reality touched my heart deeply, as I knew this was not my own imagination. It was the reality that Christ is with us no matter what we do. His love never fails us.

So, don't be surprised when battles come; they are natural and promised by God in order to strengthen you so that when you do get free, you will be able to choose to stay free. You are giving honor to God through your struggle when you pick yourself up and try again and again. Keep persevering!

The Battle of the Wills

I went to a lot of the 12 step meetings. During an Overeaters Anonymous meetings the group reads the first three steps of Alcoholics Anonymous. Step One: "I admitted I was powerless over food and my life had become unmanageable." Step Two: "Came to believe that a power greater than myself could restore me to sanity." Step Three said to "Made a decision to turn my will and my life over to the care of God, as I understand Him". This last step appears to be very simple and easy to do; but it's not for an addict! It somehow meant I had to give up controlling my life. Ugh!

Many times at Utah even though I could be doing "fine", all of a sudden I would get a crave to go binge and purge, and the nagging urge wouldn't seem to cease unless I filled it's craving. I screamed, *Don't binge, Katie!* I would then play tug-o-war with my will and vacillate back and forth for several long minutes until I made my decision to feed the hungry beast.

Most people without an eating disorder would see that healthy eating and living is the best choice and we would simply make the right choices and do it. Yet, why did I choose the opposite direction so many times? This very question always puzzled me. I felt like a Dr. Jeckyl and Mr. Hyde, resolved one minute to stay abstinent, and the next minute I had my head buried in food. At the moment I binged, it felt good and releasing, a sort of a rush and calming at the same time, but later, after the let down, it didn't seem worth it all.

I later understood that it was also because my self-will *wanted* to do it. Try to understand this with me. My will was convinced that the bulimia was the best thing for me. For so long I didn't really *want* to stop bingeing and purging. I certainly tried to, and the better part of me did want to stop. Somehow *my will* was *consenting* to all of this; and that is what needed to change.

Although I didn't think this consciously, deep down I had learned that if I binge and purge I would escape any inner tension and bad feelings and thus feel better. And if I focused on my bulimia, I didn't have to face any pain that I felt in my family and at school. I didn't have to feel disappointed, lonely, hurt, angry or anything bad. I disappeared in this rush of bulimia and avoided growing up. Thus, my will decided that it was a good thing for me.

Then, after a few years, the bulimia became sheer habit and these original motivations to binge and purge were buried alive. Unconsciously, I was still running from those grade school and high school feelings and fears, even though they were no longer serving me as an adult. The challenge was now to grow up—to be willing to act as an adult.

It was very significant to uncover those original motivations so that my will could consciously reject them. As I recognized and let go of what kept my will turned towards food, it freed me to choose to eat well. I had to work at letting my will choose ways that were blessings to me, not curses.

So in making our wills conform to God's, we must try to find out *why* we are choosing destructive habits. What is motivating you? It's probably something that you may not be aware of. There is a reason, and it's not just because you like food!

I had to work to convince my heart and mind that it was of more benefit to me to stop bingeing and purging rather than to continue. It took time for me to unravel what was motivating me to stay bulimic. Only when I became aware of what was fueling my self-will to continue could I begin to replace it with an understanding that it was better for me to not binge and purge.

Let me give you an example. I spoke with a girl with bulimia who courageously admitted that she didn't want to stop, even though she knew it is harmful to continue. I commented that it was probably because the bulimia was helping her achieve certain things that were important to her. I may have been wrong, but to me it all seemed so clear.

Her parents were having a lot of problems—her dad was drinking heavily and her mom was not there for her as she needed because she was a medical doctor with a full time practice. Her parents knew of her bulimia and she was in counseling at the time but things hadn't changed at home. Why was she doing this to herself? Possibly she was attempting to deal with her pent up emotions but also her addiction was getting her parent's desperately needed attention—*finally.*

If she stopped, she would be back to where she was before the bulimia: sad, alone, and helpless to fix anything and in deep pain. She was also getting her righteous anger out about the injustice in her family, maybe not in a healthy form, but in the "best" way she knew how. Now she could at least feel some control in what was happening in her family and maybe even fix the problem if all worked out, as her subconscious will had planned.

The only real uncomfortable part was that her track coach wouldn't let her run until she gained twelve pounds. As a result, some of her friends were treating her differently because she had bulimia and was so thin. Yet, her desire for her parent's love and affection seemed to be the primary need in her life. Her out of control feelings and self-hate possibly stemmed from her failure to fix the problem. I wondered if the burden in her heart for them signified to her that it was her task to solve the family's chaos and be their savior. She just wanted their love and care and her parent's happiness, even if it meant she would be destroyed in the process.

Perhaps subconsciously she hoped this might get them all into counseling, focus their eyes on the true problems and maybe make the family a home once again. Yet, I explained that there were better ways to achieve that goal and the negative effects of housing an addiction could affect her for many years in the future. Yet nothing her counselors or I could say would make her stop bingeing and purging. She had to convince her will that it was more beneficial to stop than to continue in the addiction. To do that she had to deal with her relationship with her family and the can of worms that was there.

When I was in a similarly situation during my bulimia, to facilitate a change in my will, I had to be honest and ask myself: *Do I really want to change? What are the consequences if I don't binge and purge? How will my family and friends relate to me differently if I choose to let God change my character? Am I ready for the difference in relationships if I become more vulnerable to people?* I needed to get deep down, gut honest as to what I was really thinking and feeling. There was a comfort in my sickness since I had lived that way for so long and I had to move past that.

I remember saying, *Katie, I want to be more relaxed around people, more myself.* That was a really great desire! I wasn't changing because deep down I didn't *want* to be more relaxed around people. I was more comfortable living isolated and self focused. I found many people's personalities irritating and wanted to stay away from getting too involved with them. I was afraid of being more vulnerable to rejection if I was really myself, or that someone might get too close for comfort, or be attracted to me in ways I was not comfortable with.

Thus, to avoid risking, I subconsciously kept the walls of self-centeredness and protection high, letting them down only for selected periods of time. I used to beat myself up for not being able to be relaxed in front of others, and of having such a hard time to really be myself—but as I understood the origination's of my actions it gave me compassion for myself and a tool to move past it.

We must *will* to do the will of God. Once I answered *why* I was doing it, I was freer to choose how I was going to deal with the situation. I could still choose the food abuse, but it became more of a choice than a compulsion.

During the days when the volcano rumbled and I felt the eruption of negative thoughts and urges to purges beginning, I would need to drag myself to a safe place, like my bedroom, a chapel, or someplace away from food. And in that spot, I would try to slow down and calm myself by talking compassionately while calling out to God for help, or calling a friend on the phone. Here, in this crisis, I could work at talking things through with others and myself and examine more deeply what I was thinking and feeling.

When I was feeling extreme anxiety or a panicky felling, I would go on a walk, journal, visit a friend or go to the library, simply to calm the torrent of feelings down so to not fall into the cycle—whatever it took. I tried to do anything, but to binge. Many times amidst those efforts I would still turn to food, but I was slowly building better habits.

Another thing that helped me to strengthen my good will was to go to the Sacrament of Reconciliation. I was able to confess to the priest, who represented Jesus and all the people I was hurting through my addiction, the ways I had failed in relationships, my self-destructiveness, and my unwillingness to stop bingeing and purging. Even though I don't think I was entirely ready to give up the bulimia, in all honesty I confessed my unwillingness to stop and declared with as much of my heart as I could, my desire to be right with food. I needed God's grace to bend my will towards His higher will.

Once in prayer, I felt that these words were an encouragement from the Lord for me and maybe they will also speak to you: *I will help you conquer your self and show you who you really are; the part who chooses hurtful ways isn't who I made you to be, that's not "you". No, I've made you to be the delight of my heart and of other's hearts. Let me reveal to you who you really are. You are my joy! Little one, don't be afraid to draw near, even though you feel filled with darkness, bitterness, and anger. Draw near to Me. Only I can relieve the pain in your heart. I love you!*

No More Diets!

Diets certainly never helped me get well, nor did trying to eat only healthy food. Maybe others have been successful with these tactics, but they only made me crazier. Yet I did need to learn to eat balanced meals, something I hadn't done for those past eleven years. When I was in the convent, we ate balanced meals with no snacks in between and ate sweets only on Feast Days. Although it was difficult to do at first, I became used to it quickly and began to enjoy their meals. This gave me a good foundation with which to build. Over those years, my metabolism returned to normal and my weight stabilized.

The majority of Americans don't get adequate vitamins in their diet. We are a fast paced, quick easy-bite society. Many people who struggle with an eating disorder have nutritionally satisfied their bodies to an even lesser degree, and are thus craving essential nutrients.

Now I basically eat whatever I want and can maintain a healthy weight. I don't have any great tricks to teach anyone, because I don't do anything out of the ordinary! To be honest, I don't pay much attention to food anymore. My natural inclination now is to eat fairly healthy and I'm so grateful for that. But the way I eat now has taken time to develop and lots of healing from the Lord.

Listed below are tips that helped me during the time that I was obsessed with food and couldn't stop bingeing and purging. They are certainly not a formula for anyone to become abstinent. Some may not work for you, but others may. Remember that you are your own story, so do things in the way that is best for you. Listen to your heart, it will tell you which way to improve the eating habits. One day you will be the one sharing your thoughts with others!

Again though, let me remind you that fixing only the food habits is not the solution. Our emotions, thoughts and spiritual dimensions need to be healed in order to be fully free.

Meal Time Tips

- Set the table nicely for the meal. Put a flower on the table to brighten things up.
- Try to get away from emotional eating. Calm yourself down before a meal like with soothing music.

- Make mealtimes a special time. If possible, eat with someone and not alone.
- Decide what to eat before the meal, preferably the night before, and try to stick to it.
- Sometimes, it was too overwhelming to make out a whole day's menu, so make the plan only until 1 PM.
- Be creative and make the food presentation look appetizing.
- Begin to recognize your triggers. For example, *Well, maybe 1-2 donuts won't hurt. I can handle just that.*
- Take smaller bites and chew your food well. Savor each bite.
- Take breath breaks from eating to just relax your body, and enter into conversations with others.
- If you are eating alone, take time to just day dream a bit, so to lower the intensity of the mealtime.
- Look at the colors of the food you are eating—the texture and shape.
- After a meal, coach yourself through it to keep it down, even when it was a healthy meal. Try to go into your quiet room and just relax, practice feeling satisfied with a healthy meal even though it had several hundred or a thousand calories. Retrain your mind to think, *This is good for you.*
- Practice feeling what hunger growls and what fullness feels like. Remain in that feeling and experience it.
- Focus not on the food itself, but on food as a blessing to your body & spirit.
- When you go to a restaurant, practice feeling peaceful amidst the array of fatty food options. I used to feel panicky and just order quickly, knowing I would purge after the meal. I discovered if I waded through the torrent of the feelings of the urge to purge, I could make good decisions from the menu that I felt comfortable with. Even restaurants can be safe places.

- Beware of buffets. Now, I rarely eat from buffets because I never eat my moneys worth there. Delight in a normal sized quality meal.
- If you do decide to have a buffet, take only a little of the things that look good, savoring each bite.
- Rekindle the sensations of fullness and taste. I had shut those off over time.
- I had to turn on those mechanisms of fullness and taste and I asked forgiveness from myself for turning that off. Then I spoke life into those body parts instead of death.
- Retrain your body to eat slowly.
- Really affirm yourself for getting through the meal. Another victory!
- Try to bless any food you eat. It will help put food in its proper perspective: Food is meant to help nourish our bodies, minds and spirits.

Tips When You're Bingeing

- Practice deep breathing before a binge to alleviate any tension. Take breaks along the way to just relax and to breathe deeply.
- If you secretly eat someone else's food, tell them or just replace it.
- Practice denying your gratification. If you do end up going on a binge, try for example, to make yourself wait ten minutes until you take the first bite. Then, tell yourself you will wait another five minutes until you eat the second or third part of whatever you bought. Or before you procure the food, put it off. Say, *In fifteen minutes I'll go eat the stuff.*
- Instead of buying your favorite cookies, buy a different brand that is less tasty.
- If you do vomit, drink a lot of water afterwards to neutralize the acid and brush your teeth. Care for yourself as a wounded soldier after being in battle. Continue

to proclaim to yourself, *Sorry for doing this. One day you will be free of this!* And believe it!

- Before you binge, listen to your body and ask it, *What do you want to eat? What are you craving? Is it pineapple? Well, maybe you need a bit of Vitamin C. If you're craving steak maybe you need Iron. Craving cheese?* You may need some protein. Give your body what it needs and try to eat just one nutritious meal a day. Some people binge because they don't have the vitamins their body needs.
- Try giving up a binge food. For example, after the police confronted me for shoplifting on bulk food, I gave up bulk food. At another time, I said, No more Jax donuts. These were small but significant achievements.
- If you do go on a binge, challenge yourself to chew every bite really well and taste the food. Ask yourself how it all tastes. You may become more sensitive to your bodily needs and eventually find yourself saying, *I don't want to binge on that; it doesn't taste good!*
- When you eat a "no-no food" like a donut, examine the flood of thoughts that scream, *Oh, well, I've blown it today. I might as well binge!* Instead think, *OK a donut isn't bad. It's not the best choice, but I've got to accept responsibility for my choices.* It can be a normal part of a meal. You can stop here and decide not to purge or eat any more.
- Really try to relax your body. Everyone holds tension in different parts of his or her bodies. Now that I am free of bulimia, I can see that I hold a lot of tension in my stomach. I never used to feel this tension because I ate over the feeling. Now, I know that when I feel nauseous, it's usually because I am anxious about something. When I have a strong craving for sweets, I am running from something that is causing me anxiety. Get to know your body and what the cravings mean.

Eating Etiquette

- Practice leaving a little food on your plate. Just a bite or two. Buy an ice cream and calmly throw a fourth of it away after you're satisfied, saying, *That was enough. I don't need anymore.* Remember, fake it until you make it! Try to learn to feel what it means for your body to be satisfied. You have turned off the sensation feeling for so long so give yourself time.
- When I would walk by a bakery or into a restaurant and see goodies in the window, make yourself look at the food, relax your body, and say, Y*ou could eat all of that food if you wanted to. Look at it. Think how that would make you feel physically, so full, bloated, and fat. Think how horrible you feel after you purge. I deserve better. I can do better. You know, I don't really want that food. I have control by saying NO to that.*
- While I was in Ireland in missionary training, my friends and I would go to town and do "food aromatherapy". It originated one day as we walked by a bakery without a penny in our pocket. The wonderful aromas would sweep under our noses causing us to stop and cling to the bakery window with both hands and face. None of us had money to spend on a treat so, we took deep breaths in, letting the aroma fill our lungs and stomachs. Over and over we did this saying to each other, "MMMMmmmm! That was good! Oh, I feel full...boy that was a good cake and cookie!" As we kept faking this, we actually became satisfied! I got over the craving, and was calm again. It worked!
- Sometimes this "aromatherapy" doesn't work, and in those times, or in times when you want to give yourself a treat, buy just one of something. One chocolate truffle, or one donut or one scoop of ice cream. This is normal eating.
- If there is something on sale, don't say, *I should just to get*

two. Listen to your body, you probably "need" only one!
- Sit down to eat. I was so used to eating and hiding my food. Look around while you eat and enjoy the beauty around you.
- After a meal, take at least fifteen minutes to relax. Watch TV, visit with someone, or daydream somewhere, or just do whatever.

Day by Day Tips
- Try to start the day calmly. Often having a quiet time of reflective prayer relaxes our body, mind and spirit. Even if you are planning in your mind to binge, just try to put yourself in God's presence before it all, asking for His help and protection and for His desires to be in your heart. You can pray this even if you go ahead and binge.
- Exercise for 20 minutes three times a week, trying not to over-exercise which can be another way of "purging". Yet do it in a way that serves your body.
- Drink six to eight cups of purified water each day. Not only does it fill you up, but also it cleanses your system and is good for you!
- Before going into a supermarket, make a list of what you need to buy. Discipline yourself to stick with that list and not rationalize that you will bless your roommates by buying that tub of ice cream.
- Dancing in a room alone in your own expressive ways can release tension and affirm who you are, expressing deep feelings.
- Developing new talents, new forms of art and athletics can be a response to filling the cravings for food and can serve to be new ways of relaxing our mind and body.
- Take time to thank God at the end of the day that He was with you through all that happened.

Facing the Harshness of Relapse

No matter what our story of bulimia is, or how well we adapt the above "practical eating tips", I suspect we have all experienced relapses in one form or another. I don't really even like that word because it connotes a negativity. Falling is actually a part of learning. Nonetheless, for lack of a better word, I will refer to reverting to old bulimic habits as relapsing.

If deeper issues are at the root of our problems, why should we focus on improving our food habits at all? This question is valid, but I found that in my recovery there was a place for practicing better eating habits, even though it took a long time to normalize them. If we are not willing to make efforts to change our eating habits and give up the control of food, progress will be stifled in dealing with inner issues. By having even short periods of abstinence, we allow ourselves to be more vulnerable and we thus can more easily receive healing. Nonetheless, even amidst months of bingeing and purging up to fifteen times a day, God worked in my heart to heal the roots of my addiction.

There is no way I could count the many, many relapses I went through. I used to waver back and forth wondering if I should call myself a "recovered bulimic" after thirty days of abstinence, then only to humiliate myself the next week and say I was just a, "bulimic" because I fell back into purging. Yet, those thirty days were a victory and I wanted to not forget that. After I kept relapsing, I gave up on the "recovered" preface, yet I continued to long to be able to truly say that. I was also distraught that my identity seemed wrapped up in the fact I was a bulimic. It was always, "I'm Katie a bulimic", not "Katie, a person who is struggling to overcome bulimia and who would one day be free."

When I left the eating disorder hospital, I was determined not to purge. My main concern was what the staff and others would think if I relapsed. I really wanted to stay clean.

I wanted to be free and to live once again, but my self-esteem was so low that there was a part of me that didn't want to get better. I didn't even believe it was possible. It was as if I wanted to punish myself for being bulimic and causing all this trouble and worry to my family and friends.

I don't know if I was ready to give up the habit at that time since I enjoyed it to some degree, despite its horrors. It was my loyal friend, or so it seemed. What would I do without my "friend"? It was as if I needed to give myself time to grieve the future loss of this close confidant, to prepare my mind to live a life without bulimia before I finally let go of it. When I would have a normal day of eating in the hospital or in the first few days after I was released, it seemed boring; there was no excitement to the day. I began to wonder if I was also addicted to the emotional highs and lows that went along with the cycle.

As a few days passed after leaving the hospital, I was eating fairly well, one...two...three days passed without purging. Yet I didn't seem to be feeling as wonderful as I had expected an abstinent person would feel. I began feeling very melancholic and somewhat depressed and wracked with anxiety. Plus I was fighting off cravings to binge and purge like a person with mosquitoes in the Amazon. And since patience was never my virtue, after seven days of abstinence, I rationalized that I could handle bingeing and vomiting just one time and then after that one purge, I would get back on track and remain abstinent forever and ever.

I convinced myself I needed that one fix, just one little one since it had been forty-nine days since I had purged. I rationalized; *It'll do me good to do it one last time. Then I'll remember how much I hate it.* Deep down what I was saying that I miss the high I get from bingeing and purging; it's too hard to be depressed. And so, I did it again.

Yet how could I have expected to be other than deeply depressed? I had a back up of unexpressed feelings that I had never dealt with and my system had been shocked and I had never learned to feel comfortable with being depressed, lonely, and angry or really anything. I had to keep reminding myself what a Twelve-step friend taught me, "There is no way out but through". Life isn't intended to always be filled with extreme highs. We must learn also to remain even keel, and live through the "blahs".

This stage in recovery reminds me of a Richard Gere movie called, "Mr. Jones". This manic-depressive man loved being on his highs because he got a lot done. Even during his depressive low stages there was some familiar benefits gained. Finally he sought the much-needed medical and psychological help for his illness. Yet as he took his medication, he realized that he no longer experienced those wonderfully addicting emotional highs. Life was no longer exciting as he knew it. Nor could he wallow in his low - lows. But he was now what society called "normal". So, unable to take that "torture" of being emotionally stable, he chose not to take his medication and to stay sick, which eventually led to his suicide.

The highs obtained from bulimia are different from Mr. Jone's emotional highs and lows but the parallel is still the same. The heightened state of anxiety and inner turmoil is somehow released through an obsessive action of eating or self-destruction. So, when there is no bulimia to relieve the tension, the person is left only with the heightened anxiety and the overwhelming emotions.

In contrast to Mr. Jones, I never experienced the highs and lows of emotions when bulimic; instead I chose to remain even-keel—numb. I was never really sad when something tragic happened, nor was really excited when something really good happened. I kept at an even keel. On the outside I looked happy, but on the inside I was dead.

Certainly I had been addicted to the effects of the bulimia itself. It had both a calming yet rushing effect. I was addicted to that surge and release of the inner tension. In the midst of a cycle, I felt so chaotic inside; yet at the same time I was strangely in control. I was scared to be grown up by adopting more civil eating habits; I'd rather just stay a kid.

After those seven days after the hospital, I, like Mr. Jones, had relapsed. Shame had become my middle name once again. Maybe I was addicted, like Mr. Jones, to my sickness, and even to my inner shame. It was very humiliating to face the hospital staff the next Tuesday, along with my hospital friends, yet I wonder if that humiliation somehow reinforces that sick part of me that said I was bad? From my perspective, people who had committed the relapse mistake seemed to be spoken of as juvenile delinquents—touched with kid gloves. Since I received that scarlet mark, it was like I didn't belong to the group. I felt like I should be like a dog with the tail in between its legs.

It takes much humility and courage to face others when in the midst of a relapse. The first reaction is to retreat and to isolate. Then as an outlaw, the person must hide out until they get their act together; or better yet, find another group who doesn't know them, join them, and start over. This feeling of shame can be overwhelming.

Yet, I remember when my hospital friend, Sharon, came to our group after relapsing when she left the hospital. I felt anything but shame for her! She was not dealt with kid gloves, and no one shunned her, but actually loved her all the more. I thought she has so much self-respect that she has the guts to come today. That's great for her, but could I be that honest?

After leaving the hospital and being often in relapse, I decided to attend support group meetings. It was so good to meet with other people with bulimia and anorexics as I felt kindred spirits with them and received encouragement primarily by the fact that they were being honest with how they were feeling and struggling. I was afraid to admit to them that I was really struggling, but when I heard others talking about their problems, it gave me the strength to say to admit that I was in the heat of a relapse.

I had to learn to not get discouraged or apathetic with the amount of falls (and I had many!), but instead, to take on an attitude of learning from each one, and to use what I learned to help the next fall be less harsh and one step closer to the end. It seemed I would get a few episodes of two weeks free from purging with bingeing still occurring, then go back onto the purging. Then a few months later I would get thirty days, falling again after that. Later, I found myself going for two to three months without purging and bingeing. Until finally, one of those three months turned into a full year!

I kept looking at my abstinence from a positive perspective instead of beating myself up for falling back into it. Finally it gave me courage to say, *NO, I don't want this habit in my life at all, ever again! One day at a time I can commit to being free of this. It's not helping me anymore and I am ready to give it up.* If I hadn't appreciated those small victories of two, four and eight weeks, I would have been more difficult to have the bigger ones. Pat yourself on the back after a day of eating normally, even if it was only one meal that you ate well. That's victory!

Celebrating the "small" victories of abstinence was so helpful. (There is actually no "small" victory when it comes to abstinence; every day is a celebration!) My friend, Barb, gave me flowers on my first year anniversary of no purging. Later, on my third year anniversary, I was too embarrassed to celebrate because I thought, *Katie, you're over it. What will people think if you tell them it's my third year of abstinence from bulimia! They won't understand. They think the whole problem is gross anyway.* So, I celebrate or even really acknowledge that I was formerly bulimic.

After those three years, I had a period of a week when I

was in Brazil working in a house for children with AIDS. As the stress mounted because of various surrounding factors, my desire to purge strongly returned, even after being absent for several years. I fell back into purging for a week. I had learned to find out what was buried and causing me to binge thus I was able to stop and deal with the feelings that were built up. And it did.

I had dealt with other deep core issues several years before, which helped me to learn how to communicate my feelings and to go to God for help. Resultantly I was able to get out of this relapse much easier than in years past. Although I purged only a few times that week, it was horrible to be back into the grips of bulimia.

I really believe that if I had been humble enough to celebrate with some close friends who understood the importance of celebrating that third year, and thanked the Lord for my victory, I wouldn't have had that week of relapse. So, please, *celebrate!*

CHAPTER NINE

Hope Amidst Suffering

Bulimia was the direct result of my decision to avoid facing my inner pain and confusion, and of depending solely on my own strength to live my life. It was an addiction that caused even more suffering because it consumed and distorted my entire life.

The suffering that accompanies recovery, however, can be redemptive. To redeem something means to buy back what is lost, but at a higher price. God is creative and all-powerful and so He can *redeem* the suffering in our every-day lives. So while God didn't cause the abuse, addiction, or hurtful events that happened in my life, He certainly used them.

As I know He did with me, He grieved and cried with you as you were sinned against by others and He weeps with you now as you bury your head in the toilet. As St. Paul writes, "where sin increased, grace overflowed all the more." (Romans 5:20) Therefore, while God is crying with you, He is also pouring out His healing and grace for you to be strengthened. It is paramount that you not let your heart become hardened. Many people accuse

God, but His intentions are always good; never does He have bad thoughts of us!

Still the *Whys* leave us dumbfounded? Why was I enabled to overcome bulimia, and others are still out there bingeing and purging? Why? They tried just as hard as I did. Obviously from our human perspective, life is not fair at times, and we do not have all the answers that will satisfy our difficult and deep questions. What I have concluded, though, is that this life is short and one day all who have chosen God will be together in Heaven.

While I was in Africa, my heart ached as I witnessed the poverty and disease of those beautiful people. If I had numbed myself with food or self-destruction I would have never had the privilege of experiencing their pain, nor could I have helped bear their burdens. Amidst our own pain and suffering, let us be courageous and not try to push it away, for suffering is truly the best school of love.

Mother Teresa of Calcutta has also taught me so much about the value of suffering. She said,

> Anyone who imitates Jesus to the full, must also share in his passion. Because we do not pray enough, we only see the human part. We don't see the divine. And we resent it. I think that much of the misunderstanding of suffering today comes from that—from resentment and bitterness. Bitterness is an infectious disease and cancer, an anger hidden inside. Suffering is meant to purify, to sanctify, to make us Christ-like.

She even goes as far as calling suffering the "kiss of Jesus". It is quite an amazing truth, isn't it?

May you continue to find strength to confront your own inner hidden sufferings, no matter how overwhelming they may be. May you be filled with courage to face the bitter pain wedged within your innermost being, knowing that you will become stronger, as you continue to unashamedly face your battle and to allow in the healing touch of Jesus. May you grow in humility to accept help from the Bread of Life whose flesh is "true food" and whose blood is "true drink." (John 6:35,55) And may you invite God into that tired, wounded part of you and gently ask Him to heal your broken heart, knowing that He will do it.

A Blessing in Disguise

It may sound odd to most people when they hear me say, "I'm grateful for my years of struggle with bulimia." Truly, what a blessing in disguise it has been since it has taught me so much about life, God, others, and myself. As a result of struggling to end this hellish insanity, I was forced to adopt a new lifestyle, a new way of thinking, feeling and relating. Even looking back on the humiliation, inner anguish, and distorted good times of youth caused by my years of bulimia, I can honestly say I am so grateful that I went through it. I'm a better person for having walked through the years of recovery and for learning new ways of living and loving through the process.

This thought might sound very strange to you, but it's true. If it weren't for the "gift" of having bulimia, I would never have endured the challenge of becoming more vulnerable to my family and friends. Nor would I have ever learned to be aware of my feelings and to understand myself to the extent that I do now. And I certainly never would have understood how much God the Father, Jesus and the Holy Spirit want to be in the center of my life.

In my total helplessness, I was forced to humbly accept the grace and care of God, as well as other people. Thus, along with St. James I can now say, "Consider it all joy, my brothers, when you encounter various trials, for you know that the testing of your faith produces perseverance. And let perseverance be perfect, so that you may be perfect and complete, lacking in nothing" (James 1:2).

Maybe it seems impossible for you to be grateful for something that is destroying your life. During the thick of the battle, I didn't *feel* grateful. Yet I somehow knew that by working through my bulimia, I would emerge a better person.

God *wants* us to come to Him when we are broken, wounded and needy because He is the Great Healer. A mechanic knows his machine and what makes it run well; he knows its strengths and weaknesses. I wouldn't think to bring my car to a computer store to get it fixed. No, I would bring it to the best, most cost-effective mechanic near my home. Therefore, where else would I go to seek healing? God knows us best, and He leads us to and works through others such as trained counselors, nutritionists, as well as those who help support and restore us spiritually.

I love this promise: "Now to Him who is able to accomplish *far more* than we could ever ask or imagine, by the power that is at work within us, to him be the glory in the church and in Christ Jesus to all generations, forever and ever. Amen." (Ephesians 3:17-19) God can and will do this great work in you of overcoming your addiction! May you, "confidently approach the throne of grace to receive mercy," (Hebrews 4:16) trusting that you are on the road to freedom!

Who Am I?

I am a person who has always had a passion to make a difference in the world. I long to see that my presence can have a permanent impact on other people's lives. This is a God designed passion built into every man and woman, whether each is aware of it or not. To do this to the full, we need to be real men and women who live like the unique people we are specially created by God to be. For many going through recovery from an eating disorder, the challenge to be able to relax and to be ourselves is something we deeply long for. We long to just cut loose of the mold and be our true selves in a society that beckons us to be Barbie doll cutouts.

In our society, where our "heroes" often value an image of outward perfection and material satisfaction as the means to true happiness, learning to face life without this bodily goal standing before us is a challenge, but it is truly a challenge worth pursuing. While I still make an effort to remain healthy, I no longer am obsessed with outward perfection and now am able to expend more energy focusing on the inward, beautiful parts of my personality, and to more fully develop the talents God gave me.

In the late 1977 the world experienced the death of two great women within the span of a week. I happened to be on a plane heading toward London when it was announced that Princess Diana was killed in a car accident. During my layover in the London airport, the atmosphere was one of utter shock and sadness. The British had lost their beloved princess, Diana. Many Americans, who lack that connection with the concept of a royalty, were touched by Diana's life, feeling as if they too were a part of the Royal family. Time magazine says, "In a way, she was more royal than the Royals. She was the image every child has of a princess" (p. 37 of September 8, 1997). God rest her soul.

Less than a week later, the world experienced the death of another treasured woman. Mother Teresa of Calcutta was truly a woman who loved God and her fellow man with all of her heart. During her time on earth she was a Princess of the King of Kings—of true Royalty—and now she is experiencing the reality of Heaven's magnificence.

Are you not God's Princess or Prince? Although this is an unseen reality, it is nonetheless true, and in Heaven you will fully perceive it. The Bible says many things about those of us who have accepted the gift of being His daughters and sons:

- "Do you not know that your body is a temple of the Holy Spirit within you, whom you have from God, and that you are not your own?" (1 Corinthians 6: 19)
- "As proof that you are children, God sent the spirit of his son into our hearts, crying out, 'Abba, Father!' So you are no longer a slave but a child, and if a child then also an heir, through God" (Galatians 4:6).
- "God created man in His image; in the divine image He created him; male and female He created them" (Genesis 1:27).
- "You formed my inmost being; you knit me in my mother's womb. I praise you so wonderfully you made me; wonderful are your works! My very self you knew; my bones were not hidden from you" (Psalm 139: 13-15).
- "And I have given them the glory you gave me, so that they may be one, as we are one, I in them and you in me, that they may be brought to perfection as one, that the world may know that you sent me, and that you loved them even as you loved me. Father they are your gift to me" (John 17: 22-24).
- "I will not reject anyone that comes to me" (John 6: 37).
- "So whoever is in Christ is a new creation: the old things have passed away; behold, new things have come" (1 Corinthians 5:17).

Who will you believe? Let us replace the lies in our minds with these truths.

When we are filled with truth, it frees us to dream about our future and to seek God's understanding of what mission he has created us for; for we all have a specific purpose in life. In order to foster a dream, we need to have a sense of self and to know where we are going—we need to have a vision for our lives. As we identify our gifts and share our talents, our identity becomes more solid.

When I was in grade school I used to dream about what I wanted to be. I usually changed my mind every month, but at one point I thought it would be really cool to be a trash collector. No one thought that was a very appealing job, but I thought it would be a great opportunity to be outdoors, hanging onto the back of a big truck while helping people out by cleaning up the street. I'd heard this was a well-paying job that would eventually allow me to purchase the Colorado horse ranch I wanted!

Sadly, as the bulimia progressed I increasingly shut off dreaming about my future. My willingness and spontaneity to think about the exciting and endless possibilities for my life were dying. I had become so focused on my bingeing and purging that I had developed tunnel vision. After one round of bingeing and purging, all my energy was spent figuring out how to overcome the next cycle, and I was afraid to risk taking on any responsibilities because of the fear of how my bulimia would impair my performance.

If I were offered a job, I had to first consider whether I would fail as a result of my constant bingeing and purging. I questioned whether I could even concentrate on the responsibility that the job would require. Hence, disillusioned with myself, and later too tired to even try to get free from the bondage, I had no motivation to dream about what I wanted to be when I grew up.

It is quite clear, therefore, that the bulimia robbed me of my spontaneity. I feared that if I acted freely, letting down my walls to have fun, people would think I was doing too well, and if they thought that, they wouldn't reach out to help me. I was that needy inside.

So hand in hand with having a dream, goes the faith that one can do one's part to attain it. In my case, to preserve my sanity amidst the constant cycle of bingeing and purging, I chose not to dream but to just exist, and to merely survive day to day. I kept hoping that I would just wake up and it would all have been a bad dream.

What I didn't realize yet, though, was that a vital element in aiding the stopping process was to risk allowing myself to *hope* once again for good times in the future, and to allow myself to thirst for God's merciful hand to help me emerge from the pit of destruction. I wanted to one day be able to live the Gospel and life to the fullest.

I knew I had to de-intensify myself and learn to laugh again. Since it didn't come naturally anymore, I had to "practice" having fun, and felt unnatural doing it, but today I love to dream and to laugh! I pray that for each of you God will release His joy within the depths of your being because having fun is the best medicine, and vital to the cure.

In allowing myself to laugh and dream, a passion for life once more began to emerge. *The Wounded Heart* defines passion as, "The deep response of the soul to life: the freedom to rejoice and to weep...it requires open-hearted, other centered, reckless involvement. Passion is tasting pleasure with delight, brokenness with tears, and evil with hatred" (p. 213).

God has made us passionate beings that we may enter in and participate in the lives of others, feeling their joys, sorrows and disappointments—feeling so tenderly about our fellow brothers and sisters that we are able to both rejoice and weep with one another. I have to say that it has been truly exciting for me to learn to express these deep feelings and to really get to know who I am! There is so much more to live for than just food! Let us seize the day!

Pursuit of Excellence

Yet how can we seize the day and pursue excellence if we keep struggling with food so badly? Are we not also included in this universal call to holiness emanating from the core of the Gospel?

Yes! The most beautiful, loving, awesome Creator

creates you and me so that we can live in an incredible intimacy with Him, and in relationships of love with one another. Whether we admit it or not, we are created with this desire to be at home with the One who loves us more than we can imagine. That's why we need to be healed and set free from all the wounds and wrong thinking that block our hearts and minds from seeing reality and experiencing this great Love. The pursuit of holiness is simply the willingness to receive and enter into this gift of Love, and Jesus is the one who makes His Bride free and pure so she can be able to enjoy and enter into this sublime relationship. That's the work of recovery.

Holiness is definitely for everyone. Everyone needs to recover from one thing or another because we're all in the same situation of needing to heal from sins we have committed or from others' sins against us. God thirsts for friendship with us, and there are no exceptions.

St. Paul urges us to, "Strive for peace with everyone and for that holiness without which no one will see the Lord" (Hebrews 12:14). Now, this striving for peace and holiness is our sanctification process. Let us look at the big picture of this sanctification process, for it can also give us encouragement to persevere in our walk of recovery. Verse 17 from 1 Corinthians 3: 10-17 talks about the motives of our works being purified on "the Day," and says, "If someone's work is burned up, that one will suffer loss; *the person will be saved, but only as through fire.*"

Look at those last words, "saved, but only as through fire". Recovery can sometimes feel like a "fire". It certainly did for me, particularly during the times I made good decisions to deny myself food and to adopt better tools for coping, or when I made myself vulnerable in ways I had never dared to before. That to me was fire.

Sanctification is God's preparation of His people—His family—to be ready to live with Him forever. Unfortunately, the reality that we fall short of perfection is painfully clear to us all. Amidst the frustration of our frailty and sins, I think God would probably say, *"No problem, don't worry. I'll help make you holy by giving you my Spirit which will convict you and change you and make you pure so that when you die, you can look Me in the eye and we can embrace one another with such passion! I'll get you ready to be able to live forever in my presence. Don't ever forget how much I love you!"* In God's mercy and love, He longs to purify us from bulimia, and from so much more!

My tendency was, and still is sometimes, to transfer my perfectionist striving onto my relationship with the Lord, but when I realize how He loves me—how he longs to be united with me, it drives me to reach out to Him more and to *want* to please Him. Then, I also want to love others because they are made in His image and likeness, and I more urgently desire to be rid of all obstacles that keep me from that love. Taking the time to pray then does not become a chore, but is transformed into my greatest opportunity to receive love and grace and strength for the day.

Maybe all you are able to do is to keep the hope alive in your heart that you will one day be free and able to love yourself, God and others. Know that that is enough. Simply offering yourself to God right where you are is the most loving and powerful thing you can do.

Wherever you are right now, don't be afraid of your passion for life, or of striving for excellence; it's *you.* I pray that you are able to break loose and to let yourself sing what is deep inside your heart. You have many talents and creativity that are waiting to be expressed. You have nothing to lose and the fullness of life to gain—go for it!

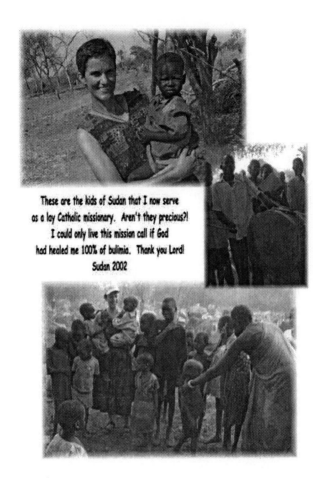

These are the kids of Sudan that I now serve
as a lay Catholic missionary. Aren't they precious?!
I could only live this mission call if God
had healed me 100% of bulimia. Thank you Lord!
Sudan 2002

CHAPTER TEN

Prayers of Love

I believe that the journey of recovery is a way of praying. Prayer is a form of communicating our deepest desires to God, of trying to transcend the bondage of our self so to reach union with the One who can set us free to be fully alive. Certainly the anguish and soul searching of recovery fits that definition.

Even through the times of intense frustration and anxiety, of uncontrolled sobbing and of numb-nothingness, we are in prayer if we are seeking to be free of what is troubling us. Prayer's forms are infinite as God is. As I progressed farther down the road of recovery, I learned that prayer is also being quiet, just being still and learning to "be".

I meet many people who were involved in ministry of some sort before the whirlwind of dealing with their incredibly wounded hearts. Now they needed to deal with the issues blocking them in their relationships and are unable to continue the ministry they were used to. They feel lost, disappointing to God and others now that they are not "saving souls" on the mission field.

The good news is that in our brokenness, we may even

be more effective in bringing the grace of salvation to the world than by preaching itself. Here are some enlightening words from St. Sr. Faustina of Divine Mercy,

> My daughter, I want to instruct you on how you are to rescue souls through sacrifice and prayer. You will save more souls through prayer and suffering than will a missionary through his teachings and sermons alone. I want to see you as a sacrifice of living love, which only then carries weight before Me. You must be annihilated, destroyed, living as if you were dead in the most secret depths of your being. You must be destroyed in that secret depth where the human eye has never penetrated; then will I find in you a pleasing sacrifice, a holocaust full of sweetness and fragrance. And great will be your power for whomever you intercede. Outwardly, your sacrifice must look like this: silent, hidden, permeated with love, imbued with prayer (Diary, #1767).

Much of my healing from bulimia has come through quiet, gentle, or groaning and wordless moments with God. It's great that prayer does not always have to involve words, particularly when we are so broken and unable to express our burden; at times, silence and groaning conveys the most precious words. Maybe this is true because in the silence we must be vulnerable. And if we make ourselves vulnerable to Him, we will find Him.

Mother Teresa of Calcutta once said, "To be able to pray we need silence—silence of the heart. We complicate prayer as we complicate many things." The more we seek to slow down and to "be" in God's presence and the presence of those around us, the more free we will become. There it is that we can experience being loved just as we are-completely and passionately. To achieve this goal, we must spend quality time daily in God's presence. That's key.

I didn't learn this quiet prayer overnight. Before I left for the Franciscan University, I lived in a half way house for recovering addicts run by a wonderful group called Women Aglow. They really helped provide a stable spiritual environment amidst the inner chaos we all lived in. I was in too much pain to pray with words. Every cell in my body was hurting. I had no idea what I needed since I saw myself as a soldier in shell shock unaware of what my real needs were. I didn't even have energy to run away from God. From my will, all I could pray was, *here I am, God. I need You. Help me. Heal me...*

The ladies of Women Aglow prayed with me for the baptism of the Holy Spirit (Acts 19: 1-9). Although I had the Holy Spirit in me and received Him at Confirmation in my parish, I knew there was more; and I saw it in these women when they prayed. They laid their hands on me and asked God to pour out His Spirit and baptize me with the gifts I needed, including praying in tongues. When we are baptized in the Holy Spirit, God gives us many gifts and even if we can't pray in tongues out load, we can certain grown in the spirit. There is such power in this type of prayer. My hunger for God grew even deeper after this and it was a significant changing point in my recovery.

It was there at the halfway house that I became more aware of my need to slow down inside and learn to listen and be quiet. I started by telling myself I would be quiet for five minutes. Five minutes didn't seem too hard of a challenge, so I sat down, said a little prayer, and closed my eyes. Immediately thoughts interrupted my silence—*What's that noise? Be quiet, Katie—you're supposed to be silent! My nose itches. I wonder how long this has been...*My five minutes of silence lasted less than three seconds!

After trying that a few times, I figured my goal was set a bit too high, so I instead tried it for five *seconds*. I know that sounds silly, but for someone who has been damaged by the constant distraction of bulimic thought and all the effects of that lifestyle, being "silent" inside seems impossible. So I begged the Lord to help me be quiet. I sat and pictured Jesus sitting right beside me, humbly teaching me how to be silent. I closed my eyes and focused on Him. One. Two. Three. Four. Five seconds...I did it! That was wonderful! That first step was all I needed to begin. Little by little the periods of silence began growing the more I practiced this type of prayer.

I found that I had to take the advice and example of so many of my well weathered Christian friends and have a daily prayer time. As long as I committed to something regularly, even if it was only 10 minutes, I saw the fruits of my growing relationship with the Lord. It is so easy to brush of spending quality time with Jesus, but it is our food to eat from His Word each day. In time, we will see our hunger for relationship increase. I would have never imagined that I could spend as much time as I do now in prayer; and still I long for more of Him!

Learning to just "be" in God's presence has been one of the sweetest experiences in my life for it somehow frees me from the attachment from unhealthy things-like food. For in His presence, there is such a peace and quiet joy that nothing can replace.

The Healing Power of Jesus' Body and Blood

Jesus' precious Body and Blood have healed me of my wounds. I have met this Jesus in the quietness of my heart, through the touch of other people and in many other sweet manifestations. I have also physically touched Him. I'd like to share with you this particular way He has touched me.

Attending the Franciscan University of Steubenville brought a new and fresh season of healing into my life. That first semester, I had a lot of extra time on my hands since my classes were not time consuming thus I got to spend a lot of time in chapel and reading spiritual books.

It had been one year since I had completed the eating disorder hospital program and although I had come a long way, my heart was still needy of a lot of healing. I was bothered only occasionally with bingeing and purging but it was still a constant, daily battle to not fall full force back into it. After many years of purging, I was so sick and tired and wanted it to finally end. I didn't know how else to finally kill this lingering monster within. I had tried every avenue to stop, never seeming to find a lasting way.

I soon began spending time sitting in the Lord's presence in front of the tabernacle where the Body of Jesus in the form of bread is reserved after Mass. I had nothing really to say to Him as I sat before Him; certainly God knew the desires of my heart. I instead needed to just "be" in His presence, not doing anything. I needed to learn to rest. Deep within, I always felt I had to *do* something for Him in order to fully please Him. Although I knew this isn't what He expected, I still felt this nagging urge to do something productive.

The more time that I sat in the presence of Jesus, the more I grew in understanding how right it was to just let God love me for who I was, not for what I could do. As those weeks of that first semester moved on, I was learning to let Him move me, like the leaves in the wind. I would spend about two hours or more a day just sitting before Him, letting Him heal my wounded heart.

Even though it was so wonderful, it was so hard to let go in His presence! It took time, courage and my deliberate will to just stay there and really relax. So often my heart felt like it was in 100 pieces. All I could do was to sit and wait for Him to touch the ugly side of myself that cowered in shame; and to my surprise He did.

Many times tears would pour out of my eyes and I would find myself sobbing for unknown reasons, exposing the woundedness of my heart. Although it was painful to let these emotions out, there was a joyful release that followed each of these times because deep healing was taking place through the silent tears. Through precious times like these, I began experiencing an inner release that was long in coming.

As I spent those months silently in front of Jesus in the Tabernacle of the chapel, I watched my confidence grow, various insecurities vanished without my effort, and I developed deeper relationships with friends. Although I still binged and purged every so often that year, the inner healing that took place was a basis for being able to finally be freed of it that following year.

What was really happening was that I was allowing myself to be loved by this Great God, my Father. This confidence of being loved then provoked a response in the depth of my being to want to worship this wonderful God. I wanted to sing awesome songs that declared how great He is. I wanted to spend time talking to him in prayer because I felt so loved by this God who made me and knew how to totally heal me of the bulimia. This relationship with God replaced other loves like food, caring what people think and materialism. I began to really love my Father in Heaven!

There is a relationship between the word "waiting" in silence, as in Isaiah 40:31and what it means to worship God. "They that wait on the Lord will renew their strength, they will soar as with eagle's wings; they will run and not grow weary, walk and not grow faint." We usually think of waiting as sitting at a long traffic light waiting for it to turn green. In this verse it instead means, "to bind together by twisting".

This kind of waiting is a form of worship, for it demands a lifestyle of depending on Him with our whole being as we lean upon Him with our entire personality, intellect, will and emotions. And this is true spiritual worship. And for those seeking total healing from bulimia, waiting is part of the journey.

When I am intertwined with God, my problems, fears, or burdens don't weigh me down like they used to. I instead hope in God. And if they do weigh me down, I know to whom I can go in prayer to lay my burden down.

Through our faith in Him, we receive the grace, which is His willingness to work on our behalf, to do whatever He asks us to do. It gives us a confidence that when in Christ's power, we can even move mountains! And we all know that this deliverance from bulimia is like a huge mountain in our lives! We can do "everything through him who empowers us" (Philippians 4:13).

So be encouraged that within the recovery process you are being taught how to love God and to give your life to Him and to come home to your family in the biggest sense of the word. You are invited to wait until your full recovery comes; and really our "full" recovery and transformation of our whole personality and being won't be until heaven where we won't have to struggle with our fallen nature at all!

Although sometimes agonizing, waiting will produce a strength that we could never have imagined! You will be freed to be the woman or man that you have always dreamed of being; not perfect, but healed of many things. The pain you are now agonizing through will turn into the most glorious, amazing jewel of true freedom.

For God loves you more than you can ever imagine, and He has a wonderful plan for your life. He will unite all your agony with His that He endured on Calvary and that He is enduring by helping to carry your cross of bulimia. Hang in there and have hope!

Daddy, I'm Home!

Boldly facing my hurts, disappointments, and my need for reconciliation opened me to a deeper relationship with others and God. It led me to God's grace, healing and forgiveness, which were vehicles for restoring the damage that had been done. Working through those hurdles allowed me to better trust and confidently depend on God to protect me, provide for me and lead me.

This process has also helped me accept and love my own parents more deeply, knowing we all have our faults and failings. There are so many wonderful memories I have with my Mom and Dad that certainly far outweigh any weaknesses, but those few memories needed to be brought to light and healed.

Parents are meant to demonstrate and reveal God's character to a child. Father's are typically the ones who instill the virtues of deep confidence, a daring boldness, one's femininity, particularly as that has to do with a child's relationship with God as Father. Despite any shortcomings and wounds in my parents, they loved me very much and have reflected God's love and provision in many incredible ways. I admire my parents and all the ways they served us kids. Even if they were ideal parents, there would still be areas I needed to grow and be healed in so to better understand God's character and love for me for they are only human vessels.

The key for my healing has been to be really gut-honest with what is going on inside, and to let go of the facade that I am strong and that I have it all together. It's our job to try to be open to work through any blockage we encounter. Instead of just acting like we are good holy Christians, it's better to be holy (whole) by being honest in saying, *I don't want to be more intimate with You, God. I don't know why, but help me to understand why.*

Isn't it awesome that God wants to help us in our weakness? We don't have to be someone we're not around Him!

He really *is* our Father. The more I discover who God is; it makes me want to be free to give Him permission to come deeper into my life. I need God to be my Father. I need family and community. We all do whether we like to admit it or not.

Our Father also has motherly qualities, as it says in Isaiah 49:15, "Can a mother forget her infant, be without tenderness for the child of her womb? Even should she forget I would never forget you. See, upon the palms of my hands I have written your name." He certainly wants to nurture us and feed us as a mother does.

God has also given me human fathers and mothers, sisters and brothers to reflect His character, so that I can get to know Him through other people's care. In addition to my own mom and dad, God has given me friend-family members who to lead me closer to Himself.

Integral to my final healing from bulimia was discovering the richness I had in Mary the Mother of Jesus, who is also my mother. In September 1989 at the Franciscan University, I felt challenged by other student's devotion to Mary to check out what they believed. I asked, "Why do I need *her*? It's just me and You, Jesus!" Yet, I strongly felt the Holy Spirit's prodding to accept her as *my* Mother, in the same way that Jesus gave her to John, "Behold your mother" (John 19:26), and the way Jesus accepted her as His mom, making her the Mother of God.

After much struggle and prayer, by faith I prayed, *Holy Spirit, if this is of You, I accept to let Mary be a mom to me and to lead me closer to Jesus through her example and prayers.* The coming months marked a recognizably deeper depth in my prayer life and understanding of Jesus' suffering and passionate love for me. I understood more deeply His humanity in such a deeper way that was not merely coincidence, but what I perceive as a direct correlation to my growing relationship with Mary my mother and Mother of all Christians. It was as if I got to know Jesus more as a mother would her son.

What I found very interesting is that it was at this point that my first significant time of abstinence from purging came—September 1st, 1989. The month before that day, I had begun grappling with accepting her as my mother and it was in that month that I was able to take that deeper step of surrendering as I had described earlier in this chapter. After I made a decision to let Mary be my Mother in whatever way the Holy Spirit intended, I experienced a significant lasting break from that bondage to binge and purge. It was as if a chain was eternally broken.

Make whatever conclusions you want, but I believe that one of the "finishing touches" in my recovery was in letting myself be a part of my spiritual family in a more full sense—particularly letting myself be spiritually cared for by God in a motherly way through a human mother, Mary.

We also have family in the Body of Christ who intercedes for us. "The fervent prayer of a righteous man is very powerful." (James 5:16) The prayers of my older brothers and sisters on my prayer team on earth and in heaven help me to receive more of God's grace to follow Christ more sincerely.

Hebrews 11 lists the great men and women who have fought the good fight and then, *"Therefore*, since we are surrounded by so great a cloud of witnesses, let us rid ourselves of every burden, and sin that clings to us, and persevere in running the race that lies before us, while keeping our eyes fixed on Jesus, the author and perfecter of our faith, who for the joy set before Him endured the cross." (Hebrews 12: 1,2) We certainly are one family in Christ.

The word, "Catholic" that we Christians pray at the end of the Nicene Creed prayer means, "international family bond." With the confidence that I have such a great family supporting me, I now am more able to allow myself to be weak. When people don't like me at times, and disapprove of me and even reject me, I can remember that I've got big brothers and sisters who don't think I'm a jerk and are standing behind me. Plus, of course my God will *never* desert me!

We are created with a desire and need for family. Building friendships has helped me to overcome the great fear of sharing myself and being free to be myself. We are not meant to go it alone.

Welcomed Home

Some of you may be familiar with the Prodigal Son story in Luke 15, but I'd like to tell it to you in a different version. I'll call it "The Trying to be a Worthy Son to His Merciful Father" story. Whatever name you give it, it really proclaims the story of the Father's grace and mercy. No matter how far we've strayed or how low we go, it never changes the truth that we always have the Father's house to return to. Always waiting to let us sit on His lap is our Father, our God who is Love. Everything originates from the Father and everything will end there, too—if we accept the never-ending invitation.

This is a parable that many of us have lived out consciously or unconsciously in our mind. Grab a cup of coffee, snuggle up with your blanket and listen to me tell this story...

A man had two sons, and the younger son said to his father, "Father give to me the share of your estate that should come to me." The Father was hurt because in Jewish homes if a son would ask this of their father before he died it was tantamount to saying, "Drop dead, Dad!" Nonetheless, with a broken heart the father divided the property between the two sons and gave the younger son his portion.

After a few days, the younger son collected all his belongings and set off to a distant country where he squandered all his inheritance in a life of rebellious living. When he had freely spent everything, a severe famine struck that country and he found himself in dire need. So he hired himself out to one of the local citizens who sent him to his farm to tend the pigs.

How he longed to eat his fill of the pods on which the pigs fed, but nobody gave him any. He thought, *Even my Father's hired servants have more than enough food to eat, but here am I dying of hunger. I wish I had not sinned by leaving my father as I did. He must think I am the lowest, worst person! I can't believe he will forgive me after all I've done.* He thought further; *I know what I'll do! I will prove to him that I am good. If I work very hard to show him this, then he will take me back!*

So he found some seeds for a small price and traveled part way home and worked hard to buy a small field were he planted some seeds. After two years his crops doubled. Then he thought, *I'm sure this is the beginning of my fortune.* My father will be so proud of me! But I will work harder to make sure. Ten years later he had earned a small fortune and had a surplus of cows and sheep on his farm. He said to himself, "I have now earned enough that I think my father may consider me worth to be his son again." Yet he was fearful of returning home and taking the chance that he might be rejected. So he labored for six more years to ensure the forgiveness for which he so longed.

Then eighteen years after he left his father, now with graying hair, he walked home, bringing with him many gifts for his father. While he was still a long way off, his father stopped what he was doing to see who was coming. He caught sight of his son and was filled with love and compassion! He still recognized his son despite the changed appearance, as he knew his son well and had looked at his picture everyday hoping he would return.

With that, he ran to his son, embraced him tightly and kissed him all over his face. "You're home, my son!" Not hearing his father's excitement and love, his son quickly interjected, "Father! I have sinned against heaven and against you. I no longer deserve to be called your son, but I have brought you cows and sheep as gifts and ten sacks of grain on a donkey to prove to you I am good and worthy to be forgiven and called your son once again!"

With tears in his eyes, his father held him even more firmly and said, "My son, my son, you are the greatest gift of all! I have waited eighteen long years for you to come home. It's broken my heart everyday not being close to you. A messenger told me you had squandered your inheritance the first year and I was hoping you would come home back then. I knew you must learn the hard way. My heart has ached not having you near these last eighteen years. Now I am so happy you are home! You did not need to earn my love for it has always been there for you no matter how low you fell. These cows and sheep are nothing in my eyes, only you are! So come, feast! We will celebrate that you were dead, but now you are alive! You were lost but now you are found!" Then the celebration began!

Your heavenly dad is saying the same thing to you right now. He says,

> It's broken my heart to have you gone from home for so long! I love you more than you'll ever know! I gave my son Jesus to be killed so that I could be your father and you could know what it is like to be my child! Let Me heal the wounds your own family members or other men or women may have unknowingly, or even overtly inflicted on you. Let me heal you so that you can enjoy my love!

Your heavenly dad is saying the same thing to you right now. He says,

It's broken my heart to have you gone from home for so long! I love you more than you'll ever know! I gave my son Jesus to be killed so that I could be your father and you could know what it is like to be my child! Let Me heal the wounds your own family members or other men or women may have unknowingly, or even overtly inflicted on you. Let me heal you so that you can enjoy my love!

CHAPTER 11

Freedom is Yours!

Do you really believe you be completely freed from the cycle of your eating disorder? The answer to this fundamental question will paint the pathway of your recovery.

I have tried in this book to encourage you that you don't have to settle for a recovery shadowed by a consistent suppression the urge to purge. Nor do you have to diet for the rest of our life in order to measure up or down, as the case may be. It's true that the standard of thinness in this society bombards us from every angle, but we can chose whether we want to play that game. I have tried to retell my story and the key elements of my healing, incomplete as it may be, to encourage you with a few points that may help you in your recovery.

Unfortunately, there exists no formula for recovery, but there *are* several key elements that need to be explored if a person wants to experience freedom. To summarize, key elements of my recovery include the following:

- Learning to recognize and express the emotions that I had numbed.

- Learning to recognize the lies I was feeding myself and then replace them with truth.
- Learning to be at home within my own body and with food and understanding who I am.
- Understanding the hidden purpose the bulimic behavior was serving.
- Building a community of support by becoming vulnerable and real with friends and family.

Nonetheless, as vital as all of these elements are, they're not enough to curtail the entire forceful blow from bulimia. There is another vital ingredient: The need to heal the deep wounds in one's heart. This can only come about by experiencing an alive, transforming relationship with the Father, Jesus and the Holy Spirit. Flowing from a person's baptism into the Church and in the Holy Spirit we have the channel of grace needed to receive that deeper healing.

Flowing from my relationship with God, I needed to:

- Understand God's heart for me so that I could trust Him to heal me.
- Invite God to transform and heal the wounded memories, thought processes and emotions and the concept of who I am in Christ and as a woman.
- Allow God to be the center of all parts of my life.

As I came to understand who God really is and how much He really loves me, then other areas of my life fell into place. I could then believe I was fully loved; that He had a specific purpose for my life. Then I could admit I was not ultimately the one responsible and capable of healing myself. When I understood that it was okay to admit I was powerless to free myself from the grips of bulimia, I was free to accept His power to help me overcome it. I became willing to change my heart.

Everything seemed to flow from this understanding of God's loving heart for me. We cannot be free to live in love of self and others when our hearts are full of pain. The only place to be healed is in the embrace of God. We cannot experience healing without understanding God's feelings toward us and God's relationship to us.

As we begin to understand the roots of our eating disorder, we empower ourselves to subdue its negative forces. Thus, with the help of God's grace, the truth sets us free.

A House of Healing

I liken my healing to the building of a house. Try to draw a picture of this: The foundation is the understanding God's love for who we are and God's plan for freedom in our life. The walls are the healing of our wounds and memories. The door is our "Yes" to enter into the process of God's healing and recovery. The roof is the right eating habits and a healthy body and self-image. (Many recovery programs focus solely on this one.) The chimney is the vehicle for virtues of love, peace and joy of the Holy Spirit to flow out when the proper structural components are built. Here our ego is overshadowed by our God-given personality since we have made room for Christ to be at the center of our lives. The aroma and that which flows from the chimney and embracing the entire structure is our union with God.

Many people fall into despair during recovery because their house is still not fully built after years of struggle through recovery. This feeling of defeat may be deterred if we accept that it is a process; not built overnight. Recovery also has order. To talk about stopping our bulimic behaviors without discussing healing is similar to trying to put a roof on a house before building the walls. It just doesn't work that way.

Many people have never worked through the inner wounds, and thus forever struggle with an eating disorder. They keep distracted by their work, ministry, relationships or other addictions. Their conclusion then follows, "It's not possible to fully recover." Without submitting my wounded heart to the process of healing and all the suffering that it entails, I would never have known the full rest I longed for deep within my soul.

I've met some people who reach lower levels of freedom without dealing with all of the roots and wounds causing their disorder. Some deep roots are just too painful to experience thus they stay satisfied with a partial recovery. That is fine if they are at peace with that decisions but for me I always desired more.

For me, recovery had a higher standard. It meant getting to a point where one is free and peaceful deep within no matter the cost. It means an end to the running from that aching emptiness because a still, sweet and tranquil resting place has been found. It meant if necessary even putting my ministry and education on hold until I took the necessary time to deal with what blocks were staring me in the face. Through it all I was leaning on the arms of grace and friends who loved me, not on my own strength.

Likewise for you, the One who loves you and made you for a specific purpose holds out His hand to guide you along your pathway to freedom.

The Nightmare Will End

Your seemingly eternal nightmare can and will end because the grace and gift I have freely received is available to everyone. The only "payment" for this gift is a willingness to suffer the pain of being honest with yourself and others. It requires enduring the necessary healing so to build strong walls for your house. Although this is costly, I can attest that it is worth the price!

To acquire the gift of freedom from bulimia, you must face the pain and stumbling blocks lodged within that are holding you back. The agony of embracing and speaking the truth to yourself is worth enduring when you have hope that one day you will be free from bulimia. If you are satisfied with staying within the walls of bulimia then you are only half-alive and then cannot be at home within yourself. Coming alive and coming home is a big challenge only for the brave and courageous.

Recovery is a sacrifice. My time spent in recovery, was both a sacrifice and an investment. It is often a greater sacrifice to work through issues as we postpone our longings to be a blessing to others in some sort of ministry. Most, if not all of us, are very sensitive people who genuinely love to care for others, and it is a sacrifice to put serving others somewhat on hold until we get our lives in order. God knows the longing of your heart and honors it. The day will come when you will fulfill the ministry and job God has put on your heart. Choose to hope. So many people encouraged me with the fact that Jesus prepared for thirty years for his ministry of less than three years! Think about it!

During the first part of recovery I felt very self focused and absorbed, but it was necessary to be that way for that period of time. There is an essential season for looking at ourselves that is essential but that season will end. It's like learning to ride a bike...in the beginning, the child stares at the ground three inches in front of the tire. The hands are gripped on the handlebars as they wobble back and forth on the sidewalk. It takes intense self-focus to get it right!

I think the main reason I am so free today is because I knew my recovery was not the end goal. I knew there was life after bulimia waiting for me to indulge in. I developed an understanding that God desired incredible intimacy and friendship with me, His Bride and that it was possible for me to enjoy it. That gave me strength and courage to carry the cross and to face anything I saw about myself that needed changing. This then urged me forward to embrace God as love and to receive His love, which gave me the security to press on. I knew that whatever root sin and flaw I saw in myself that needed to change, I could bear because He has born the shame of it through the cross.

I saw my life like a cocoon. At the beginning of recovery I looked and felt like a caterpillar. If I bore the darkness of the life in the cocoon and the growing pains of developing wings, then I would one day be a butterfly. I could then fly. I would be more beautiful. I would then be free to bring life and joy to others. I wanted to get through my grueling recovery so that I could sacrifice my life in love for other people like Jesus has done for me.

Most of the insights I have received which helped me over the hurdles were realized not in counseling sessions or in the hospital, but when I took time to listen to that still small voice within. Recovery is not dependent on the right counselor or correct therapy, although these are very helpful. Much of it depends on an honest willingness to persevere through the obscurity and to be willing to allow yourself to be healed.

Your story of recovery is happening in its right time. It may take longer than did mine, or possibly much shorter. You can take whatever time you need. Whatever the timing or means, you can trust that God is forming you through your weaknesses and addictions. Keep pressing on!

I encourage you to give God permission to take you to a new level of recovery. Remember—God will never force healing on anyone. Whether we are aware of it consciously or subconsciously, we can often resist something good— even recovery from bulimia—because we perceive that that the pain to get there will be unbearable. I know I did. We can choose to stay in the comfort of our sickness and avoid giving God and ourselves the permission to let go of things that keep us in bondage.

I knew if I really wanted to be free of bulimia, and of my shame and lack of freedom, I had to be willing to be hurt again. Running from the pain is what causes the problems. I needed to learn how to live with a vulnerable heart sheltered by God's truth and love and not my lies.

A Loving Father

I want close this book with an image that may help you grasp the fact that God is there to walk you through the pain of your recovery so that you can be fully healed. Your Heavenly Father and our Blessed Mother are also hurting with you during this difficult trial.

Here's the story…a child named Annie has accidentally fallen into a deep well. With legs and arms broken, ribs bruised and face battered, she waits for her Daddy to rescue her. She knows he will. It hurts even to cry, so she lies silent and immobile, whimpering, and helplessly waiting.

When her mother and father find her, and they get things ready for the rescue: the rope to climb down on, a sheet to carry her in, a blanket to wrap her in when they reach the top and her mom intently waiting to take her in the car to the hospital. All this takes time, and her daddy shouts to his sweetheart, "Hang on! I'm coming-You'll be out soon!" and her mother works quickly to get things ready.

Finally, he slowly scales down the rope so as not to lose his grip. Once he reaches her, he so much wants to embrace her, but knows her frail body could not handle it, so he speaks calmly to her so to reassure her that he will be with her during the difficult and painful assent. "It's okay, Annie. I'll soon get you out. You're safe now with me-don't worry!"

When he goes to lift her, she violently screams as her broken bones press on her nerves and torn tissue. Her dad's careful handling and great loving care do not seem to lessen her pain as he brings her to his chest and wraps her around himself in the sheet. Tears stream down his face as his beloved daughter writhes in uncontrolled pain. Yet, seeming to ignore it, he focuses on the task of getting her up the well to safety.

Slowly, slowly they ascend together. Annie's only task is to endure what seems like torture, but what she knows she must endure in order to be free. After what seems like three hours, but is really only a matter of minutes, they reach the top to find mom beaming with a mixture of joy and pain at seeing the frailty of her little one. On the way to the hospital the girl's tears are mixed with a sigh of relief knowing she is safe with her parents again, yet desperately afraid of the agony that awaits her at the hospital.

Annie's pain was intense and she could not foresee how good she would feel once healed and recovered. But her parents did. That is why they allowed her to be subject to further wounding including the doctors and nurses, the needles, the physical therapy and of not being able to play and be like the other children for what seemed like an eternity.

After much rehabilitation and loving care, she recovered and began running and playing again. Although she now ran with a slight limp, it later served to teach her something. It was her parent's love and hope for her that motivated them to put her through such a trial. She didn't understand until she was older how much her parents actually loved her through such a hard time.

Likewise, may the Lord strengthen *you* for the journey you're on when you feel as if you can't play like the other children. May you receive hope to know that this is only a season you must endure—an investment-even though the minutes seem like years. One day you will be free to love as you so desperately long to do and to be embraced in that very love. May you hear a loving Father say to you, "I'll soon get you out. You're safe now with me. Don't worry!"

Now it is your chance to come home. Come home to Jesus—to your Father and your family. He is saying to you right now, "Come to me all you who labor and are burdened and I will give you rest. Take my yoke upon you and learn from me, for I am meek and humble of heart and you will find rest for yourself" (Matthew 11:28-29).

He really wants to walk you through all the pain you are going through and will go through in the future.

If there is anything in your heart that is not supposed to be there, I hope that my story has shaken it up. I pray that you let go of trying to control things that are not meant for you to control and put them into the hands that have created you and who loves you tenderly. When you allow your walls to come down and give permission to let your woundedness heal, you will experience the beauty of love. It is your choice to receive it. It may take time—be patient. Just wait, the freedom will come for you too.

My story is all about hope-hope for *your* life. Hope not in your ability to dig yourselves out of your pit, but to trust in a power greater than yourself—in God's mercy to bring you through the hell of your addiction. Hope that you can be freed so to be the person God has created you to be and to live the vocation and tasks that you desire to live.

Also may you have hope for the life to come, for this life isn't the goal. We've got Heaven waiting for us who believe where there is no more pain, no more tears and certainly no chance of any addictions. It's a place too wonderful to imagine!

Wait on the Lord for the joy and peace that wells up from an inner confidence that is ignited by God himself. You are too special to Him to be numbed by bingeing and purging! There is so much more to life and to who you are!

You are so unique and beautiful! God bless you!

Prayer of an Unknown Confederate Soldier

I asked God for strength that I might achieve;
I was made weak that I might learn to obey.
I asked for health that I might do great things,
I was given infirmity that I might learn to obey.
I asked for riches that I might be happy,
I was given poverty that I might be wise.
I asked for power that I might have the praise of men,
I was given weakness that I might feel the need for God.
I asked for all things that I might enjoy life,
I was given life that I might enjoy all things.
I got nothing that I had asked for,
but got everything I had hoped for.
Almost despite myself, my unspoken prayers were
answered
I am, among all men, most richly blessed.

Epilogue

I'm sitting in my room gazing out at the beautiful cherry trees in full bloom, in awe of all the wonders of God's world and especially what He has done for me. It's amazing! Just last week I was still in Africa living and toiling with my Sudanese brothers and sisters in the mission I have been serving in for the last 3 years. Who would have thought a young woman who was so ruined by the clutch of bulimia could be thriving so bountifully in a challenging war torn country like Sudan, a place so far from any comforts of American life?

"Once a bulimic, always a bulimic", and "In times of stress you will return to bingeing and vomiting", the 'experts' said. Can you not see that is flat out untrue? I'm not a bulimic anymore; I'm a child of God who is healed. I am enjoying living God's plan for my life!

I'm have not returned to the habits of bulimia or any other addiction but am striving to live a life of holiness and to grow more and more free in my own personality. I now am in closer union with the God who has freed me from those blinding chains. I am transformed just as the Gospel promises I would be.

God is far greater than bulimia. *That* is the truth.

Something I unexpectedly find is that when I return from the missions I am usually a bit underweight due to the strenuous work, the stress, and availability of only healthy foods. In fact this time I had lost a good amount of weight due to the scorching temperatures (115-120 degrees!), long days helping the visiting surgeons, organizing the people for surgeries, a bit of homesickness and again falling victim to some local parasites. Thus, since I left last month, I have had to make efforts to *put on* weight! Now *how's that* for a former bulimic to have to *try* to put on weight!

I have thoroughly enjoyed these past weeks eating the ice cream, pastries and pizza; not in a binge mode, but in a healthy, normal, savoring manner! I'm free! I am able to enjoy food without a "hang up" about my body or food itself. And even though I am thin my body fat percentage is not what it was when I was playing sports, and I am satisfied because my body is integrated into my personhood and no longer the center of my life.

Even more than the healing of food issues, I am so grateful that I have a healthy relationship with my parents, siblings and friends. Thank you, Jesus!

I lovingly send each of you my prayers. I wish I could meet with each of you and walk through your recovery with you, but this you must do alone. Your story of recovery is unique to *you*, written by the hand of the One who loves you passionately and who is behind you 100%. Don't be afraid—He will see you through to the end and never leave you. Hunger for your God-Hunger for freedom!

APPENDIX

Workbook

Some of you may benefit from discussing and meditating about these questions, or making up your own questions and letting the Word of God minister to your soul and to one another. Each chapter review has a thought-provoking quote, a set of questions and a Scripture passage. I hope this can be helpful for you or those with whom you choose to meet.

Chapter 1

Out of weakness comes strength. Our weakness is our gift from God because in it we come to know God's infinite goodness to us. It opens us up to the truth of our strength and beauty in God.

St. Catherine of Sienna

Questions:
1. Do you believe you can fully recover from bulimia? Why, or why not?
2. What do you expect to get out of this book?

Galatians 5:1
It was for freedom that Christ set us free;
so stand firm and do not submit again to the yoke of
slavery.

Hosea 6:1-3
Come let us return to the Lord, for He has torn us,
but He will heal us; he has struck us,
but he will bind our wounds.
He will revive us after two days;
on the third day He will raise us up, to live in his presence.
Let us know; let us strive to know the Lord;
as certain as the dawn is his coming,
and his judgment shines forth like the light of day!
He will come to us like the rain, like spring rain that waters
the earth...

Chapter 2

*The more faithfully we can trace the line of
our past, the more clearly we can see the line
of our present, and the more thoughtfully we
can imagine the line of our future.*

Robert Benson

Questions:
1. How has your addiction affected your work, school or everyday life and attitude?
2. Do your family and close friends know how the extent of your problem? If not, why don't you tell them?
3. Is there a dream you have, or something you feel God is calling you to that cannot be accomplished if you are still bound to an eating disorder? Write a

prayer to pave the way for this plan to be realized in your life.

Sirach 2: 1-7
My son, when you come to serve the Lord,
prepare yourself for trials.
Be sincere of heart and steadfast,
undisturbed in time of adversity.
Cling to him, forsake him not;
thus will your future be great. Accept whatever befalls you,
in crushing misfortune be patient;
for in fire gold is tested and worthy men
in the crucible of humiliation.
Trust God and he will help you;
make straight your ways and hope in him. You who fear the
Lord, wait for his mercy,
turn not away lest you fall.
You who fear the Lord, trust him,
and your reward will not be lost.
You who fear the Lord, hope for good things,
for lasting joy and mercy.

Chapter 3

The heart has reasons which reason cannot understand.

Blaise Pascal

Questions:
1. What are you feeling right now? Why?
2. How do you usually express your anger? How did you express it growing up? What makes you really blow up?
3. What truths about your past does God want you to

face right now?
4. Are you able to express your feelings to a friend or counselor? If not, what holds you back?
5. What do you think about the three A's: Awareness, Action and Acceptance in relation to where you're at in recovery?

Psalm 142
My spirit is faint within me, but you know my path.
Along the way I walk they have hidden a trap for me.
I look to my right hand, but no friend is there.
There is no escape for me;
no one cares for me.
I cry out to you, Lord, I say, You are my refuge, my portion
in the land of the living.
Listen to my cry for help, for I am brought very low.
Rescue me from my pursuers, for they are too strong for
me. Lead me out of my prison,
That I may give thanks to your name.
Then the just shall gather around me, because you have
been good to me.

Chapter 4

For you have made us for yourself, and our heart is restless until it rests in You.
St. Augustine

Questions:
1. What do you desire deep within? Can you face that hunger? Why or why not?
2. Are you afraid of facing something? Why? What will it take to get through these fears?
3. What is the deepest longing in your heart? How can

you help fulfill it?

Matthew 5:3-10
Blessed are the poor in spirit,
for theirs is the kingdom of heaven.
Blessed are they who mourn, for they will be comforted.
Blessed are the meek, for they will inherit the land.
Blessed are they who hunger and thirst for righteousness,
for they will be satisfied.
Blessed are the merciful, for they will be shown mercy.
Blessed are the clean of heart, for they will see God.
Blessed are the peacemakers,
for they will be called children of God.
Blessed are they who are persecuted for the sake of righteousness, for theirs is the kingdom of heaven.

Chapter 5

*The Resurrection means trouble for us who
are comfortable with being only half alive.*
Alan W. Jones

Questions:
1. How do you perceive God the Father? Do you feel comfortable letting God get close to you?
2. How do you feel when someone believes the best in you?
3. What does surrendering mean to you? What are some areas you're still holding on to?
4. Are you able to rest inside with a peace, knowing that you are loved?
   If not, simply ask God for that gift. What could be some of the barriers?

Isaiah 61: 1-3
The spirit of the Lord God is upon me,
because the lord has anointed me;
He has sent me to bring glad tidings to the lowly,
To heal the broken hearted,
To proclaim liberty to the captives and release
to the prisoners,
To announce a year of favor from the Lord,
a day of vindication by our God,
To comfort all who mourn;
To place on those who mourn in Zion a diadem
instead of ashes,
To give them oil of gladness in place of mourning,
A glorious mantle instead of a listless spirit.
They will be called oaks of justice, planted by the Lord to
show his glory.

Chapter 6

The fact that we crucified Him and yet have been forgiven means there is nothing we can ever do that is worse than that! If God forgave us of that, then there is nothing we can ever do, no matter how discouraged we become because of our miscues or hardships or struggles—nothing, absolutely nothing can separate us from the love of Christ... nothing!

The Healing Power of Love p. 154
by Floyd McClung

Questions:
1. Do you feel that you have toxic shame inside? How does it bind you and keep you stuck?

2. Take a moment to invite Jesus to come in and sit with you as you feel your shame. Imagine His loving, understanding eyes on you as you sit in your pain of shame. Let Him touch and heal you.
3. What curses and vows have you put on yourself? Do you want to renounce them? If not, what is the fear holding you back?
4. What do you feel like after you have asked God to forgive a certain sin? Do you experience joy and freedom and grace afterwards? If not, how do you think you can get to that point?
5. In what ways has your eating disorder or addiction been an inner rejection of embracing your life?

II Corinthians 4: 16-18
Therefore, we are not discouraged; rather, although our outer self is wasting away, our inner self is being renewed day by day. For this momentary light affliction is producing for us an eternal weight of glory far beyond all comparison, as we look not to what i s seen but to what is unseen; for what is seen is transitory, but what is unseen is eternal.

Chapter 7

The glory of friendship is not the outstretched hand, nor the kindly smile, nor the joy of companionship, it's the spiritual inspiration that comes to one when he discovers that someone else believes in him and is willing to trust him.

Ralph Waldo Emerson

Questions:
1. Do you feel that you have a lot of shame inside? How does it bind you and keep you stuck?
2. Take a moment to invite Jesus to come in and sit with you as you feel your shame. Imagine His loving, understanding eyes on you as you sit in your pain of shame. Let Him touch and heal you.
3. What curses and vows have you put on yourself? Do you want to renounce them? If not, what is the fear holding you back?
4. What do you feel like after you have asked God to forgive a certain sin? Do you experience joy and freedom and grace afterwards? If not, how do you think you can get to that point?
5. In what ways has your eating disorder or addiction been an inner rejection of embracing your life?

II Corinthians 4: 16-18
Therefore, we are not discouraged; rather,
although our outer self is wasting away, our inner self is
being renewed day by day.
For this momentary light affliction is producing for us an
eternal weight of glory
far beyond all comparison,
as we look not to what is seen but to what is unseen; for
what is seen is transitory,
but what is unseen is eternal.

Chapter 8

Knowing ourselves outside of God equals confusion and discouragement. You can't separate knowing yourself and knowing God's love and mercy. God can turn even our sin into the blessing of humility, charity and increased dependence on Him.

St. Catherine of Siena

Questions:

1. Can you admit that you are powerless to heal yourself of your eating disorder addiction? Why do you think that you can still control it?
2. Do you think self condemnation is useful for you? If not, what things can you do for yourself to defeat self condemnation?
1. Why did you or are you choosing destructive habits? What are you getting out of it?
2. Which mealtime tips were most helpful, or what are other creative ways that help you to put order in your eating patterns?
3. How do you view relapse? Failure or a learning experience?
4. What positive thing have you learned about yourself lately? Say something positive about the person on your right.

Psalm 51

A psalm of David when Nathan the prophet came to him after his affair with Bethsheba:

Have mercy on me, God in your goodness;
in your abundant compassion blot out my offense.
Wash away all my guilt; from my sin cleanse me.
For I know my offense; my sin is always before me...
Still, you insist on sincerity of heart; in my inmost being teach me wisdom.
Cleanse me with hyssop, that I may be pure; wash me, make me whiter than snow.
Let me hear sounds of joy and gladness; let the bones you have crushed rejoice.

Turn away your face from my sins; blot out all my guilt.
A clean heart create for me, God;
renew in me a steadfast spirit.

Chapter 9

God reveals himself to the little and the wounded and to each of us to the extent that we accept that we are little and wounded. He liberates us from the prison of our egoisms and the prison of our comforts, from the prison of convention which prevents us from living as free human beings and even less as children of God.

Jean Vanier, <u>Be Not Afraid</u>, p. 40

Questions:
1. Do you see any benefit in suffering through the inner pains of recovery? Is it helping you mature and heal?
2. What is the most difficult thing about recovery?
3. Do you think you will or do now see your eating disorder as a blessing in disguise? Why?
4. Which scripture about your identity spoke to you most? Why?

Psalm 139: 1-13
Lord, you have probed me, you know me;
You know when I sit and stand;
you understand my thoughts from afar.
My travels and my rest you mark;
with all my ways you are familiar.
Even before a word is on my tongue, Lord you know it all.
Behind and before you encircle me and rest
your hand upon me.

Such knowledge is beyond me,
far too lofty for me to reach.
Where can I hide from your spirit?
From your presence, where can I flee?
...You formed my inmost being;
you knit me in my mother's womb.
I praise you, so wonderfully you made me;
wonderful are your works!

Chapter 10

*Breathe in me, O Holy Spirit that my
thoughts may all be holy;*
*Act in me O Holy Spirit that my work too
may be holy;*
*Draw my heart, O Holy Spirit, that I love
but what is holy;*
*Strengthen me, O Holy Spirit, to defend
all that is holy;*
*Guard me then O Holy Spirit, that I
always may be holy.*

Prayer of Mother Teresa

Questions:
1. What helps you to keep a daily prayer time?
2. How do you see the character of God the Father? Is it related to your own Father's behavior? Pray with each other for any healing you need so to know God as He really is.
3. How is your conception of Mother in line with the character of God? Can you also let God mother you? Can you also ask Mary, the Mother of Jesus to be a mother to you and lead you to the Father?
4. What spoke to you in the story of the merciful Father?

Hebrews 4:13-16
For we do not have a high priest who is unable
to sympathize with our weaknesses,
but one who has similarly been tested in every way,
yet without sin.
So let us confidently approach the throne of grace
to receive mercy and to find grace for timely help.

Chapter 11

*Faith is to believe what we do not see, and
the reward of faith is to see what we believe.*
Saint Augustine of Hippo

Questions:
1. What spoke to you in this chapter? What most spoke
   to you while reading the book?
2. What is God saying to you in these days and teaching you?
3. Do you trust that God wants to set you free from
   your eating disorder so that you can live the vocation
   that He has created you to live? Why?
4. Consider praying the following prayer over each
   other or asking someone to pray with you:

PRAYER FOR HEALING

I say to you, in the name of the Lord Jesus Christ, that
your life is not a mistake. God made you out of the love that
He is. He called you into being at the right time and the
right place. He prepared a way for you and gave His life for
you. Your are a privilege, not a burden; a joy and a delight,
not a disappointment; you are not an intrusion, you belong.

You are a treasure just because you are, and not for what you can do.

You are one of the Father God's special children, and He delights in you.

Heavenly Father, I ask you to destroy all the lies this child has accepted and bring to the cross every destructive attitude, expectation and personality structure or habit pattern. Lord, I see you pouring you love all about this child, breathing your fresh life into his/her spirit. Wrap your strong welcoming arms about this child and invite him/her to grow into the fullness of his/her own life restfully, as God has planned for him/her from the beginning. I pray that _____'s inner child be enabled to forgive those who wounded him/her negative response to any hurts in his/her life. I pour the healing love of Jesus into the wounded spirit like a healing balm. I ask the Lord to gift you with his sovereign gift of trust and rest and peace, and to let his/her entire being be integrated with wholeness and harmony, as he/she is reconciled to being who he/she is, where he/she is.

I place the cross of Christ, in the name of Jesus Christ of Nazareth, between this child and his/her parents and his/her parent's parents all the way back on both sides, through all his/her generations, declaring that all of his/her inheritance be filtered through your cross. All dependency of evil, every curse coming to this child through his/her family line must stop on that cross. Lord, hide this child in your heart and cast light in the eyes of any powers of darkness, that might attempt to oppress or afflict of prevent his/her life. I stand in the Lord's authority against such powers.

Finally I place the Lord's blessing in the name of Jesus on this child's life. Lord melt any hardness of heart, strengthen with your might in the inner child, and enlighten the eyes of his/her heart, open door for him/her, draw him/her to your destiny, and place your mantle of protection on him/her.

1 Peter 5:6-10

Cast all your worries upon Him because he cares for you...
The God of all grace who called you to his eternal glory
through Christ Jesus,
will himself restore, confirm, strengthen, and establish you
after you have suffered a little.
To him be dominion forever. Amen.

APPENDIX

References

These books can be purchased on the web either at www.bookfinder.com or Amazon.com or any other such site. The Groups and organizations below also can be found from any search engine on the web.

Books that are helpful:

- The Secret Language of an Eating Disorder, Peggy Claude-Pierre
- The Inner Development Study Guide, Jackie Barrile
- The Monster Within, Cynthia Rawlands
- The Wounded Heart (book and workbook), Dr. Dan B. Allender and Dr. Larry Crabb
- The Father Heart of God and The Healing Power of Love, Floyd McClung
- Unbound, Neil Lozano
- Power in Praise and Prison to Praise, Merlin Carothers
- Healing for Damaged Emotions (book and workbook) David A. Seamands, Victor Books Publishing, 1992

- Health the Shame that Binds You, John Bradshaw: Deerfield Beach, FL, Health Communications Inc. Publishing, 1988
- The Search for Significance (book and workbook) by Robert McGee, Rapha Publishing, 1990
- The Weigh Down Diet, Gwen Schamblin

Associations/Groups/Hospitals

- Minerth-Meier in Patient Hospitals
- Ramuda Ranch (In-Patient), Arizona
- American Anorexia/Bulimia Association
- National Association of Anorexia Nervosa and Associated Disorders
- National Association for Christian Recovery
- Counseling seminars for abused people Dr. Allander and Dr. Crabb, Colorado Springs, CO.
- Institute for Christian Living, Riverside Medical Center, Minneapolis, MN
- Tools for Recovery, San Diego, CA
- Overeaters and Bulimics Anonymous
- Overcomers Outreach, Inc.

Miscellaneous

- Teachings on the Catholic Faith: www.scotthahn.com
- All for Him Inc. (Katie's Sudan mission site) www.allforhimsudan.com

Acknowledgements

I want to thank the many wonderful people who have walked along with me during these 10 years of writing and editing this book. Beamer, you have been behind me the longest and kept me laughing and hoping along the way! Susan and Urby you welcomed me to stay at your house to initially put it all into the computer and have since cheered me on; Cathy—you've been at my side even before the writing of the book and have seen me through as a good friend would. Martha, Zoe, Angela, Patty, Margaret, Janine, Holly and many other friends have edited, reviewed material and prayed for me to get this book out—Thanks to everyone! And thanks to my wonderful family, Mom and Dad and Sue, Carolyn and Thomas who have encouraged me to publish this and who bore with me through the years of recovery. And last but never least I thank my most awesome loving God who has done so many miracles in my life and loves me more than I can imagine and whom I know is giving this same gift of healing to millions of others. Thank you all!

Printed in the United States
80008LV00002B/37